INTERNET INVESTIGATIONS

in

Business Communication

by

Cynthia B. Leshin

Prentice Hall
Upper Saddle River, New Jersey   Columbus, Ohio

Editor: Charles E. Stewart, Jr.
Production Editor: JoEllen Gohr
Cover Designer: Julia Zonneveld Van Hook
Production Manager: Patricia A. Tonneman
Marketing Manager: Debbie Yarnell

This book was printed and bound by Quebecor Printing/Book Press. The cover was printed by Phoenix Color Corp.

© 1997 by Prentice-Hall, Inc.
Simon & Schuster/A Viacom Company
Upper Saddle River, New Jersey 07458

Netscape Communication Corporation™ Copyright

Netscape Communication Corporation (NCC), Netscape, Netscape Navigator, and Netsite are trademarks or registered trademarks of Netscape Communications Corporation. Netscape Communication Corporation has granted permission to use screen captures from their home page and to describe Netscape Navigator and its interface. Whereas Netscape's tutorial has been referred to, all efforts have been made not to copy this document.

Printed in the United States of America
10 9 8 7 6 5 4 3 2

ISBN: 0-13-495987-6

Prentice-Hall International (UK) Limited, *London*
Prentice-Hall of Australia Pty. Limited, *Sydney*
Prentice-Hall Canada Inc., *Toronto*
Prentice-Hall Hispanoamericana, S. A., *Mexico*
Prentice-Hall of India Private Limited, *New Delhi*
Prentice-Hall of Japan, Inc., *Tokyo*
Simon & Schuster Asia Pte. Ltd., *Singapore*
Editora Prentice-Hall do Brasil, Ltda., *Rio de Janeiro*

DISCLAIMER

While a great deal of care has been taken to provide accurate and current information, the Internet is a dynamic and rapidly changing environment. Information may be in one place today and either gone or in a new location tomorrow. New sites come up daily; others disappear. Some sites provide forwarding address information; others will not. The publisher and author assume no responsibility for errors or omissions. Neither is any liability assumed for damages resulting from the use of this information.

As you travel the information superhighway and find that a resource you are looking for can no longer be found at a given Internet address, there are several steps you can take:

1. Check for a new Internet address or link, often provided on the site of the old address.

2. Use one of the search engines described in Chapter 5 with the title of the Internet resource as keywords.

3. Explore Internet databases such as Yahoo, Magellan, Infoseek, Galaxy, or the World Wide Web Virtual Library, which have large directories of Internet resources on Web sites.

The author welcomes readers' feedback, correction of inaccuracies, and suggestions for improvements in subsequent editions. Cynthia Leshin can be contacted by e-mail at: **cleshin@xplora.com**

NOTE This guide presents Netscape Navigator 2.0. Subsequent updates (Navigator 2.01, 2.02 and 3.0) will have few noticeable changes for Internet navigation and communication. Navigator 2.02 has security enhancements. Navigator 3.0 has added fully integrated audio, video, 3D, and Internet telephone communication capabilities. These capabilities make it possible to hear audio, watch movies, and travel through 3D worlds without adding separate helper application software.

About the Author

Cynthia Leshin is an educational technologies specialist with her doctorate in educational technology from Arizona State University. Dr. Leshin has her own publishing, training, and consulting company. She has authored three books: *Internet Adventures — Step-by-Step Guide to Finding and Using Educational Resources*, *Netscape Adventures — Step-by-Step Guide to Netscape Navigator and the World Wide Web*, and *Instructional Design: Strategies and Tactics*. The last of these is being used in graduate programs. Her company, XPLORA, publishes the *Internet Adventures* quarterly newsletter to assist teachers with integrating the Internet into the curriculum. Additionally, she is currently writing discipline-specific Internet books and Internet-based learning activities for Prentice Hall.

Dr. Leshin has taught computer literacy and Internet classes at Arizona State University West and Estrella Mountain Community College. She currently teaches Internet classes using distance learning technology for Educational Management Group, a Simon & Schuster company. The Internet serves as a tool for teaching and communicating with her students. Her World Wide Web site is a learning resource for students and is also used when making presentations.

Dr. Leshin consults with schools and businesses interested in connecting to the Internet. Her expertise in educational psychology and theories of learning provides her with a unique background for translating complicated technical information into an easy-to-use, easy-to-understand, practical learning resource.

Preface ....

Internet Investigations in Business Communication meets the needs of professors, students, and others interested in learning how to use the Internet as a communication and information retrieval tool. This manual provides a step-by-step, easy-to-follow guide to help you use the Internet to find information and to communicate within the global community.

Effective communication is key to the success of businesses worldwide. Customer and employee satisfaction are equally tangible elements to that success. Customers' perceived degree of responsiveness and the quality of communication from a company are central to building long-term relationships. Productive, efficient, and happy employees generally enjoy open communication channels between management and staff within their organizations. Therefore, continuing knowledge of current communication tools is essential in today's business world.

Methods of communication have changed dramatically over the past two decades. Before the 1970s, communication with customers and employees was either in person, by telephone, or by U.S. mail. In the 1980s, new communication tools began to emerge with the introduction of fax machines, personal computers, computer networks, electronic mail, express mail, cellular phones, and telecommunication technologies.

No one, not even corporate giants such as Microsoft, envisioned how the Internet would change our world. No one could have prophesied that the Internet of the 1970s and 1980s based at our educational institutions would become the fastest growing communication medium of all times. Today we are experiencing perhaps the greatest revolution in communication. Some have called the World Wide Web the fourth media, positioned to take a place with print, radio, and television as a mass market means of communication.

This new medium has changed the way we work, do business, communicate, access information, and spend our leisure time. The world is being transformed by the digital revolution, and those who do not join this webolution will be left behind. The Internet is not a trend. It is like an ever-cresting wave being driven by the force and momentum of international currents, spraying its global magic from the monitor and inviting us to jump in—the world awaits. Travel, information-on-demand, and communication make the Internet a technology that is here to stay.

But we are still pioneers in exploring the uses of this powerful new tool. At home, at school, or at work, children and adults alike are fascinated with the entertainment and edification aspects of the Internet. Individuals and businesses—from Fortune 500 companies to small sole proprietorships—are establishing their links in cyberspace, browsing for new customers, new profits, a new way to do business, even a new way to live. Opportunities for commerce and the private sector to find good matches to their personal interests, in trade, and/or employment are quickly becoming unlimited.

Many companies, in fact, are turning to the Internet to find employees, believing that the people who keep up with the most current information and technology advances in their field will be the best candidates for employment. These professionals are already cybersurfing, networking with peers, researching information, asking questions, and learning collaboratively from others around the world.

And now *Internet Investigations in Business Communication* provides the foundation you need to begin using the Internet to communicate and to access and disseminate information. In this guide, you will learn about browsers, the software programs that make it possible to navigate the Internet and view multimedia resources (text, images, video, and sound) on the World Wide Web—simply by pointing and clicking your mouse.

In Chapter 4 (Chatting on the Net) you will find Internet's communication tools— listserv mailing lists, Usenet newsgroups, Internet Relay Chat (IRC), Internet phones, and Internet videoconferencing. Chapter 5 explains how to use search tools and search engines to find information on the Internet.

This guide also introduces you to many excellent business communication resources on the Internet. You will learn how to use the Internet for career planning and showcasing your talents and skills on an electronic résumé. And, most importantly, you will learn how to use the Internet as a valuable and important instrument to help you guide your personal and professional life.

Chapter 10 (Learning Adventures) provides hands-on activities for applying and using the information in this guide. Chapter 11 leads you through application activities exploring, discovering, and using Internet resources in business communication.

The Appendices add valuable information for connecting to the Internet, finding an Internet provider, and referencing electronic resources when writing a paper or report.

Your journey will be divided into two parts:

PART I: Understanding the Internet
- Chapter 1: What Is the Internet?

- Chapter 2: Guided Tour—Internet Browsers

- Chapter 3: Hands-on Practice

- Chapter 4: Chatting on the Net

- Chapter 5: Finding Information and Resources

PART II: The Web and Business Communication
- Chapter 6: Cool Business Communication Web Sites

- Chapter 7: Using Cyberspace for Career Planning

- Chapter 8: Using Cyberspace to Find a Job

Happy Internet Adventures

Acknowledgments...

The author would like to thank several people for making this guide possible:

I am most grateful to Charles Stewart for the opportunity to write this guide.

To my copy editor, Norma Nelson, for teaching me so much about book design and for her many important and useful suggestions to improve my writing.

To Professor Paul R. Timm and Jason Caldwell for their support and assistance in finding business communication resources on the Internet.

To Todd Haughton and Bob McLaughlin for their artistic support.

To Jill Faber for her input and expertise in career planning and job searching.

To JoEllen Gohr, managing editor, and all the other personnel at Prentice Hall who have transformed these words into this guide, especially those who read the manuscript and made valuable and most appreciated suggestions.

To my husband, Steve, for his continuing support and for helping to make this Internet adventure possible.

CONTENTS

Chapter 5: Finding Information & Resources   57

PART II — The Web and Business Communication   72

Chapter 6: Cool Business Communication Sites   73

PART I

Understanding the Internet

CHAPTER 1
What Is the Internet?

In this chapter, you will learn

- ➺ what it means to "be on the Internet."
- ➺ the difference between the Internet and the World Wide Web.
- ➺ Internet addressing protocol—the URL.
- ➺ the three standards used by the World Wide Web.

What Is the Internet?

in′ter·net n
1. world's largest information network **2.** global
web of computer networks **3.** inter-network of many
networks all running the TCP/IP protocol
4. powerful communication tool **5.** giant highway
system connecting computers and the regional
and local networks that connect these computers
syn **information superhighway, infobahn,
data highway, electronic highway, Net,
cyberspace**

The term most frequently used to refer to the Internet is "information
superhighway." This superhighway is a vast network of computers
connecting people and resources around the world. The Internet is
accessible to anyone with a computer and a modem.

The Internet began in 1969 when a collection of computer networks was
developed. The first network was sponsored by the United States
Department of Defense in response to a need for military institutions
and universities to share their research. In the 1970s, government and
university networks continued to develop as many organizations and

companies began to build private computer networks. In the late 1980s, the National Science Foundation (NSF) created five supercomputer centers at major universities. This special network is the foundation of the Internet today.

Computer networks were initially established to share information among institutions that were physically separate. Throughout the years these networks have grown and the volume and type of information made available to people outside these institutions have also continued to evolve and grow. Today we can exchange electronic mail, conduct research, and look at and obtain files that contain text information, graphics, sound, and video. As more and more schools, universities, organizations, and institutions develop new resources, they are made available to us through our computer networks. These networks make it possible for us to be globally interconnected with each other and to this wealth of information.

What Does It Mean To "Be on the Internet"?

"Being on the Internet" means having full access to all Internet services. Any commercial service or institution that has full Internet access provides the following:

- Electronic mail (e-mail)
- Telnet
- File Transfer Protocol (FTP)
- World Wide Web

Electronic Mail

Electronic mail is the most basic, the easiest to use, and for many people, the most useful Internet service. E-mail services allow you to send, forward, and receive messages from people all over the world, usually at no charge. You can then easily reply to, save, file, and categorize received messages.

Electronic mail also makes it possible to participate in electronic conferences and discussions. You can use e-mail to request information from individuals, universities, and institutions.

Telnet

Telnet provides the capability to login to a remote computer and to work interactively with it. When you run a Telnet session, your computer is remotely connected to a computer at another location, but will act as if it were directly connected to that computer.

File Transfer Protocol (FTP)

File Transfer Protocol is a method that allows you to move files and data from one computer to another. File Transfer Protocol, most commonly referred to as FTP, enables you to download magazines, books, documents, free software, music, graphics, and much more.

World Wide Web

The World Wide Web (WWW or Web) is a collection of standards and protocols used to access information available on the Internet. World Wide Web users can easily access text documents, images, video, and sound.

The Web and the Internet

The Web is a collection of documents linked together in what is called a *hypermedia system*. Links point to any location on the Internet that can contain information in the form of text, graphics, video, or sound files.

Using the World Wide Web requires "browser" to view Web documents and navigate through the intricate link structure. Currently there are between 30-40 different Web browsers. In this guide you will learn how to use two of the premiere Web browsers—Netscape Navigator and Microsoft's Explorer. Both of these browsers combine a point-and-click interface design with an "open" architecture that is capable of integrating other Internet tools such as electronic mail, FTP, Gopher, WAIS, and Usenet newsgroups. This architecture makes it relatively easy to incorporate images, video, and sound into text documents.

The World Wide Web was developed at the European Particle Physics Laboratory (CERN) in Geneva, Switzerland as a means for physicists to share papers and data easily. It has evolved into a sophisticated technology that can now link hypertext and hypermedia documents.

The Web and the Internet are *not* synonymous. The World Wide Web is a collection of standards and protocols used to access information available on the Internet. The Internet is the network used to transport information.

The Web uses three standards:

- URLs (Uniform Resource Locators)
- HTTP (Hypertext Transfer Protocol)
- HTML (Hypertext Markup Language)

These standards provide a mechanism for WWW servers and clients to locate and display information available through other protocols such as Gopher, FTP, and Telnet.

URLs (Uniform Resource Locators)

URLs are a standard format for identifying locations on the Internet. They also allow an addressing system for other Internet protocols such as access to Gopher menus, FTP file retrieval, and Usenet newsgroups. URLs specify three types of information needed to retrieve a document:

- the protocol to be used;
- the server address to which to connect; and
- the path to the information.

The format for a URL is: **protocol//server-name/path**

FIGURE 1.1
Sample URLs

World Wide Web URL:	http://home.netscape.com/home/welcome.html
Document from a secure server:	https://netscape.com
Gopher URL:	gopher://umslvma.umsl.edu/Library
FTP URL:	ftp://nic.umass.edu
Telnet URL:	telnet://geophys.washington.edu
Usenet URL:	news:rec.humor.funny

NOTE

The URL for newsgroups omits the two slashes. The two slashes designate the beginning of a server name. Since you are using your Internet provider's local news server, you do not need to designate a news server by adding the slashes.

URL TIPS..

Do not capitalize the protocol string. For example, the HTTP protocol should be **http://** not **HTTP://**. Some browsers such as Netscape correct these errors; others do not.

If you have trouble connecting to a Web site, check your URL to be sure you have typed the address correctly.

Do not add a slash (/) at the end of a URL such as **http://home.netscape.com** because a slash indicates that there is another path to follow.

7

HTTP (Hypertext Transfer Protocol)

HTTP is a protocol used to transfer information within the World Wide Web. Web site URLs begin with the http protocol:

http://

This Web URL connects you to Netscape's Home Page.

http://home.netscape.com

HTML (Hypertext Markup Language)

HTML is the programming language used to create a Web page. It formats the text of the document, describes its structure, and specifies links to other documents. HTML also includes programming to access and display different media such as images, video, and sound.

The Adventure Begins...

Now that you have a basic understanding of the Internet, you are ready to begin your adventure. Before you can travel and explore the information superhighway, you will first need the following:

- an Internet account

- a username and password (required to log onto your Internet account)

- instructions from your institution on how to log on and log off

Getting Started

1. Turn on your computer.
2. Log onto your network using your institution's login procedures.
3. Open Netscape Navigator, Explorer, or the Internet browser that you will be using.

CHAPTER 2
Guided Tour—Internet Browsers

This chapter provides you with a guided tour of the two most widely used Internet browsers—Netscape Navigator and Microsoft Internet Explorer. You will learn

- → how to navigate the Internet by using toolbar buttons and pull-down menus.
- → how to save your favorite Internet sites (URLs) as bookmarks.

Netscape Navigator

Netscape Navigator is a user-friendly graphical browser for the Internet. Netscape makes it possible to view and interact with multimedia resources (text, images, video, and sound) by pointing-and-clicking your mouse on pull-down menus and toolbar buttons.

Netscape Navigator (Version 1.0) was developed in 1994 by Marc Andreessen and others who also developed the first graphical Internet browser, Mosaic, at the National Center for Supercomputing Applications (NCSA) at the University of Illinois at Urbana-Champaign. It quickly became the standard and was the premiere Internet information browser in 1995. Netscape Navigator 2.0 was introduced in February 1996. Navigator 3.0 was introduced in August 1996.

Features and Capabilities

Netscape Navigator features include the ability to

- use Netscape as your electronic mail program.
- connect to Gopher, FTP, and Telnet sites without using additional software.

- read Usenet newsgroups.
- save your favorite Internet addresses (URLs) as bookmarks.
- download images, video, and sound files to your computer desktop.
- view, save, or print the HTML programming code for Web pages as either text or HTML source code.
- use forms for collecting information.
- use plug-in programs, such as JAVA, that extend the capabilities of Netscape.

The Netscape Window (page)

The World Wide Web is unique in that its architecture allows multimedia resources to be incorporated into a hypertext file or document called a *page*. A Web page or *window* may contain text, images, movies, and sound. Each multimedia resource on a page has associated locational information to link you to the resource. This locational information is called the URL.

The Netscape Navigator window includes the following features to assist you with your Internet travels:

- The *Window Title Bar* shows the name of the current document.

- *Page display* shows the content of the Netscape window. A page includes text and links to images, video, and sound files. Links include highlighted words (colored and/or underlined) or icons. Click on a highlighted word or icon to bring another page of related information into view.

- *Frames* is a segmented portion of a Netscape page that contains its own page. For information on frame use, see page 162.

- *Progress Bar* shows the completed percentage of your document layout as your page downloads.

- *Mail Icon* (the small envelope in the bottom-right corner of the Netscape page, or the Mail and News pages) provides you with information on the status of your mail. A question mark next to the mail envelope indicates that Netscape cannot automatically check the mail server for new e-mail messages.

- *Address location* field shows the URL address of the current document.

- *Toolbar* buttons activate Netscape features and navigational aids.

- *Directory* buttons display resources for helping you to browse the Internet.

- Security indicators (*doorkey icon* in the lower-left corner of the window) identify whether a document is secure (doorkey icon is blue) or insecure (doorkey icon is grey).

The Home Page

The Home Page as shown in Figure 2.1 is the starting point for your journey using a Web browser such as Netscape Navigator. Home pages are created by Internet providers, colleges and universities, schools, businesses, individuals, or anyone who has information they want to make available on the Internet. For example, a college or university may have links to information on the college and courses taught.

FIGURE 2.1
A Home Page for Intel
http://www.intel.com

Navigating With Netscape

This guided tour introduces you to Netscape's graphical interface navigational tools:

- hyperlinks
- toolbar buttons
- pull-down menus

Hyperlinks

When you begin Netscape you will start with a Home Page. Click on highlighted words (colored and/or underlined) to bring another page of related information to your screen.

Images will automatically load onto this page unless you have turned off the **Auto Load Images** found under the **Options** menu. If you have turned off this option you will see this icon which represents an image that can be downloaded.

If you want to view this image, click on the highlighted icon or on the **Images** button.

As you travel the World Wide Web, you will find other icons to represent movies, video, and sound. Click on these icons to download (link) to these resources.

Toolbar Buttons

Netscape toolbar buttons

Back: Point-and-click on the **Back** button to go to your previous page.

Forward: This button takes you to the next page of your history list. The history list keeps track of the pages you link to.

Home: This button takes you back to the first opening page that you started with.

Reload: Click on this button to reload the same page that you are viewing. Changes made in the source page will be shown in this new page.

Images: Clicking on this button downloads images onto your current page. Netscape provides you with an option to not download images when you access a page. This makes page downloading faster. If you have selected this option (found in **Options** menu—**Auto Load Images**) and decide that you would like to view an image, just click on the **Images** button.

Open: Use this button to access a dialog box for typing in URLs for Web sites, newsgroups, Gopher, FTP, and Telnet.

Print: Select this button to print the current page you are viewing.

Find: If you are searching for a word in the current page you are viewing, click on the **Find** button for a dialog box to enter the word or phrase.

Stop: This button stops the downloading of Web pages: text, images, video, or sound.

Netscape navigational buttons for exploring the Net

What's New?	What's Cool?	Handbook	Net Search	Net Directory	Software

What's New: Visit *What's New* to link to the best new sites.

What's Cool: Netscape's selection of cool Web sites to visit.

Handbook: Links you to online Netscape tutorials, references, and index.

Net Search: Clicking on this button links you to available search engines that help find a particular site or document. Search engines use keywords and concepts to help find information in titles or headers of documents, directories, or the entire documents.

Net Directory: Click on this button to explore Internet resources categorized by topic. Some directories cover the entire Internet; some present only what they feel is relevant; others focus on a particular field.

Software: This button connects you to information about Netscape Navigator software: subscription programs, upgrade information, and registration.

Pull-down Menus

Nine pull-down menus offer navigational tools for your Netscape journeys: File, Edit, View, Go, Bookmarks, Options, Directory, Window, and Help (Windows only).

File Menu

Many of the **File** menu options work the same as they do in other applications. You also have options to open a new Netscape window, Home Page, or Internet site.

FIGURE 2.2

Netscape **File** pull-down menu

File	Edit	View	Go	Boo
New Web Browser				⌘N
New Mail Message				⌘M
Mail Document...				
Open Location...				⌘L
Open File...				⌘O
Close				⌘W
Save as...				
Upload File...				
Page Setup...				
Print...				⌘P
Quit				⌘Q

New Web Browser: Creates a new Netscape window. This window displays the first page you viewed when you connected to Netscape.

New Mail Message: Opens an e-mail composition box that allows you to create and send a message or attach a document to your mail message.

Mail Document (or Mail Frame): Lets you send an e-mail message with the Web page you are viewing attached. The page's URL will be included.

Open Location: Works the same as the **Open** toolbar button. Enter a URL address in the dialog box.

Open File: Provides a dialog box to open a file on your computer's hard drive. For example, you can open a Web image downloaded to your hard drive without being connected to the Internet.

Close: Closes the current Netscape page. On Windows, this option exits the Netscape application when you close the last page.

Save as... (or Save Frame as): Creates a file to save the contents of the current Internet page you are viewing in the Netscape window. The page can be saved as plain text or in source (HTML) format.

Upload File: Click on this option to upload a file to the FTP server indicated by the current URL. You can also upload images by dragging and dropping files from the desktop to the Netscape window. **NOTE:** This command is active only when you are connected to an FTP server.

Page Setup: Click on this to specify your printing options.

Print: Click on this button to print the current page or frame. To print a single frame, click in the desired frame.

Print Preview (Windows only): Previews the printed page on the screen.

Select All: Selects all you have indicated by using the application's

Edit Menu

The **Edit** menu makes it possible to cut and paste text from a Web page to your computer's clipboard. This option can be used to copy and paste text from a page or frame to a word processing document or another application of your choice. The options under this menu are similar to what you have available in many of your computer software applications under their **File** menus (i.e., word processing, desktop publishing, and graphics applications).

FIGURE 2.3
Netscape **Edit** menu

Edit	View	Go
Can't Undo		⌘Z
Cut		⌘X
Copy		⌘C
Paste		⌘V
Clear		
Select All		⌘A
Find...		⌘F
Find Again		⌘G

■ **Undo...** (or **Can't Undo**): May reverse the last action you performed.

■ **Cut:** Removes what you have selected and places it on the clipboard.

■ **Copy:** Copies the current selection to the computer's clipboard.

■ **Paste:** Puts the current clipboard's contents in the document you are working on.

■ **Clear** (for the Macintosh only): Removes the current selection.

■ **Exit** (on Macintosh—**Quit**): Exits the Netscape application.

Select All: Selects all you have indicated by using the application's selection markers. May be used to select items before you cut, copy, or paste.

Find: Lets you search for a word or phrase within the current Web page.

Find Again: Searches for another occurrence of the word or phrase specified when you used the **Find** command.

View Menu

The **View** menu offers options for viewing images, the Netscape page, HTML source code, and information on the current Web's document structure.

FIGURE 2.4
View menu options from Netscape

View	Go	Bookmar
Reload		⌘R
Reload Frame		
Load Images		⌘I
Document Source		
Document Info		

Reload: Downloads a new copy of the current Netscape page you are viewing to replace the one originally loaded. Netscape checks the network server to see if any changes have occurred to the page.

Reload Frame: Downloads a new copy of the currently selected page within a single frame on a Netscape page.

Load Images: If you have set **Auto Load Images** in your Netscape **Options** menu, images from a Web page will be automatically loaded. If this option has not been selected, choose **Load Images** to display the current Netscape page.

Refresh (Windows only): Downloads a new copy of the current Netscape page from local memory to replace the one originally loaded.

Document Source: Selecting this option provides you with the format of HTML (HyperText Markup Language). The HTML source text contains programming commands used to create the page.

Document Info: Produces a page in a separate Netscape window with information on the current Web document's structure and composition, including title, location (URL), date of the last modification, character set encoding, and security status.

Go Menu

The **Go** menu has Netscape navigational aids.

FIGURE 2.5
Netscape **Go** menu

Go	**Bookmarks**	**Options**	**Directory**	**Window**	
Back					⌘[
Forward					⌘]
Home					
Stop Loading					⌘.
✓Featured Events - Livefrom HST					⌘0
NASA K-12 Internet: Live from the Hubble Space Tel...					⌘1
Web66: What's New					⌘2

Back: Takes you back to the previous page in your history list. Same as the **Back** button on the toolbar. The history list keeps track of all the pages you link to.

Forward: Takes you to the next page of your history list. Same as the **Forward** button on the toolbar.

Home: Takes you to the Home Page. Same as the **Home** button on the toolbar.

Stop Loading: Stops downloading the current page. Same as the **Stop** button.

History Items: A list of the titles of the places you have visited. Select menu items to display their page. To view the History list, select the **Window** menu and then choose **History.**

Bookmarks Menu

Bookmarks makes it possible to save and organize your favorite Internet visits. Opening this pull-down menu allows you to view and download your favorite pages quickly.

FIGURE 2.6
Netscape **Bookmark** menu

Bookmarks	Item	Window
Add Bookmark		⌘D
MY LIBRARY		▶
NEWS.PUBLICATIONS		▶
BUSINESS		▶
TEACHING & LEARNING		▶
BEST EDUCATIONAL SITES		▶
FAMILIES		▶
KIDS		▶
COOLEST SITES		▶

Add Bookmark: Click on **Add Bookmark** to save this page in your bookmark list. Behind the scenes, Netscape saves the URL address so you can access this page by pointing-and-clicking on the item in your list.

Bookmark Items: Below **Add Bookmark**, you will see a list of your saved pages. Point-and-click on any item to bring this page to your screen.

To view your bookmarks, add new bookmark folders, arrange the order of your bookmarks, or to do any editing, select the **Window** menu and choose **Bookmarks**.

Options Menu

The **Options** menu offers customization tools to personalize your use of Netscape Navigator. Several uses for these customization tools include:

- showing the toolbar buttons.
- showing the URL location of a page.
- showing the Directory buttons.
- automatic loading of images.
- selecting styles for pages to appear.
- selecting which Home Page you want to appear when you log onto Netscape.
- selecting link styles (colors).
- selecting your news server to interact with Usenet newsgroups.
- setting up e-mail on Netscape.

There are additional customization tools available that are more advanced. Refer to the Netscape online handbook for more information on **Options** and **Preferences**.

> **NOTE**
>
> Before you can use the e-mail and Usenet newsgroup tools available in Netscape, you will need to customize the **Mail and News Preferences**.

FIGURE 2.7

Netscape **Options** menu

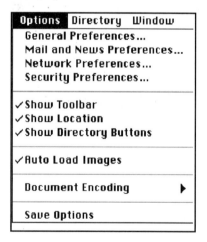

General Preferences: Presents tab buttons for selecting preferences. Each tab presents a panel for customizing Netscape's operations for your personal needs, preferences, and interests.

Mail and News Preferences: Panel for entering information on your mail and news server, so you can use Netscape to send and receive e-mail and to participate in Usenet newsgroups.

Network Preferences: Options for cache, network connections, and proxy configurations.

Security Preferences: Panel for setting security features.

Show Toolbar: If selected, the Toolbar buttons are visible on the Netscape page.

Show Location: If selected, the URL location for the page is displayed.

Show Directory Buttons: If selected, the Directory buttons are visible.

Show Java Console (Windows only): If selected, displays the Java Console window.

Auto Load Images: If selected, images embedded into a page will be loaded automatically. If not checked, images can be loaded by clicking on the **Load Images** button. Deselecting this option increases the speed of downloading a page.

Document Encoding: Lets you select which character set encoding a document uses when document encoding is either not specified or unavailable. The proportional and fixed fonts are selected using the **General Preferences/Fonts** panel.

Save Options: Click on this option to save the changes you made to any of the above options.

Directory Menu

The **Directory** pull-down menu directs you to a few navigational aids to help you begin your Web exploration.

FIGURE 2.8
Netscape **Directory** menu

Directory	Window
Netscape's Home	
What's New?	
What's Cool?	
Netscape Galleria	
Internet Directory	
Internet Search	
Internet White Pages	
About the Internet	

Netscape's Home: Takes you to the Netscape Home Page.

What's New: Click on this item to see what's new on the Internet.

What's Cool: Netscape's selection of interesting places to visit.

Netscape Galleria: A showcase of Netscape customers who have built Net sites using Netscape Server software. Visit the Galleria to learn more about how to build and maintain innovative Web sites.

Internet Directory: Same as the Internet Directory button. Links you to Internet directories for finding information and resources.

Internet Search: Connects you to many of the best online search engines.

Internet White Pages: Links you to tools to help you find people connected to the Internet.

About the Internet: Links to resources to help you learn more about the Internet.

Window Menu

The **Window** menu makes it possible for you to navigate easily between your e-mail, Usenet news, and Bookmarks windows, and to see and visit places you have already traveled.

FIGURE 2.9
Netscape **Window** menu

Window	Mon 12:
Netscape Mail	
Netscape News	
Address Book	
Bookmarks	⌘B
History	⌘H
GRAND CANYON National Park Home Page	

Macintosh **Window**

Windows **Window**

 **Netscape Mail:** Click on this option to access the Netscape e-mail program.

 **Netscape News:** Click on this option to access the Usenet newsgroups.

 **Address Book:** Displays an Address Book window for use with the e-mail program.

 **Bookmarks:** Displays bookmarks and pull-down menus for working with or editing your bookmarks.

 **History:** Displays a history list of the pages (their titles and URLs) that you have recently viewed. Select an item and press the **Go To** button (or double-click) to revisit the page.

Microsoft Internet Explorer

Now that you're familiar with Internet navigation using Netscape, you will be able to transfer that knowledge to the use of other Internet browsers. Most browsers have similar or the same navigational tools in the form of toolbar buttons and pull-down menus. Microsoft Internet Explorer is another widely used and highly sophisticated browser that is integrated with the Windows 95 operating environment. Explorer is the primary Internet browser for America Online (AOL) and CompuServe. Notice in Figure 2.10 how similar the navigational tools are to those of Netscape's Navigator.

FIGURE 2.10
Microsoft Internet Explorer window

Navigating With Internet Explorer

Toolbar buttons and pull-down menus are your Internet navigational tools when using Internet Explorer.

Toolbar Buttons

 Open: Accesses a dialog box for typing in URLs, documents, or folders for Windows to open.

 Print: Prints the page you are viewing.

 Send: Information services for using Microsoft's fax, e-mail, Netscape Internet transport, or Microsoft's Network Online Services.

 Back/Forward: Takes you either back to your previous page or forward to the next page in your history list.

 Stop: Stops the downloading of a Web page: text, images, video, or sound.

 Refresh: Brings a new copy of the current Explorer page from local memory to replace the one originally loaded.

 Open Start Page: Takes you back to the first opening page.

 Search the Internet: Click this button for a list of search services to help you find information on the Internet.

 Read Newsgroups: This option brings up a list of Usenet newsgroups available from your Internet provider or college university.

Open Favorites: Click this button to see a list of your favorite URLs.

 Add to Favorites: Click on this button to add a favorite URL to your list.

 Use Larger/Smaller Font: Increase or decrease the size of the font on the page you are viewing.

 Cut: Removes what you have selected and places it on the clipboard.

 Copy: Copies the current selection to the computer's clipboard.

 Paste: Puts the current clipboard's contents in the document you are working on.

Pull-down Menus

Pull-down menus offer navigational tools for your Internet exploration. Some of the options are similar to the toolbar buttons: File, Edit, View, Go, Favorites, Help.

NOTE

The pull-down menus will *not* be discussed or shown *unless* their functions differ significantly from the discussion of pull-down menus under Netscape Navigator.

File Menu

Explorer's **File** menu provides options for connecting to new Internet sites, printing Web pages, creating desktop shortcuts to your favorite Web pages, and to finding information about the page you are viewing.

FIGURE 2.11

Explorer's **File** pull-down menu

 **Create Shortcut:** Select this option to create a shortcut to the current page that will be placed on your desktop.

 **Properties:** Provides you with general information about the page you are viewing, including security information.

Edit Menu

The **Edit** menu offers cut, copy, and paste options as well as a find command for keywords searches.

FIGURE 2.12

Explorer's **Edit** menu

View Menu

The **View** menu options help you to determine how your Explorer page will appear. **Toolbar**, **Address Bar**, and **Status Bar** provide options for viewing or not viewing these Explorer tools.

FIGURE 2.13
Explorer's **View** menu
with active tools checked

Go Menu

Among the **Go** menu options are moving forward to the next page in your history list or backward to a previous page.

FIGURE 2.14
Explorer's **Go** menu
displaying navigational options

Start Page: Takes you back to the opening page you started with.

Search the Internet: Takes you to search tools for finding information on the Internet.

Read Newsgroups: This option takes you to Explorer's news reader for Usenet newsgroups.

Favorites Menu

Explorer's **Favorites** list is the same as Netscape's Bookmarks or what other browser's refer to as a *hotlist*.

FIGURE 2.15
Explorer's **Favorites** menu

Add To Favorites: Select this option to add the URL of a Web site to Explorer's Favorites list.

Open Favorites: Use this option to select a URL for Explorer to open.

Help menu

The **Help** menu provides help with using Internet Explorer.

FIGURE 2.16
Explorer's **Help** menu

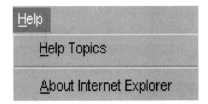

FIGURE 2.17
Explorer's **Help** Contents panel

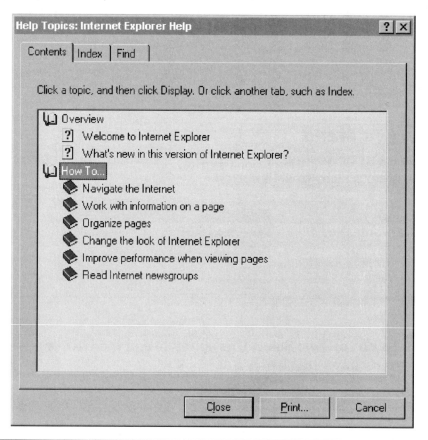

NOTE

Internet browsers such as Netscape Navigator and Internet Explorer support many additional capabilities such as electronic mail, Usenet newsgroups, Gopher, FTP, Telnet, and downloading and viewing image, video, and sound files. For a more in-depth discussion and practice using these features, refer to *Netscape Adventures—Step-by-Step Guide to Netscape Navigator and the World Wide Web* by Cynthia Leshin and published by Prentice Hall, 1997.

CHAPTER 3
Hands-on Practice

- -

In this chapter, you will practice using Netscape and/or Explorer for

- ➡ navigating the Internet.
- ➡ organizing and using bookmarks.
- ➡ exploring the Internet.

- -

Practice 1:
Browsing the Internet

In this guided practice you will use Netscape Navigator or Explorer to

- • connect to World Wide Web sites and Home Pages;
- • use pull-down menus and navigational toolbar buttons to navigate World Wide Web sites; and
- • save bookmarks of your favorite pages.

1. *Log onto your Internet account.* When you have connected, open the Netscape Navigator or Explorer browser by double-clicking on the application icon.

Netscape Navigator Icon   Microsoft Explorer Icon

You will be taken to a Home Page. Notice the Location/Address URLs in Figure 3.1 and Figure 3.2. This Home Page may belong to Netscape Communications Corporation (**http://home.netscape.com**) or Microsoft (**http://www.microsoft.com**), or it may have been designed by your college or university. Look at the top of the Home Page in the Title Bar to see whose Home Page you are visiting.

URLs are a standard for locating Internet documents. Highlighted text on Netscape pages contains built-in URL information for linking to that information. You can also type in new URL text to link a page.

FIGURE 3.1

Netscape Navigator toolbar buttons

FIGURE 3.2

Microsoft Internet Explorer toolbar buttons

2. *Begin exploring* the World Wide Web by using Netscape's toolbar buttons and pull-down menus. Click on the **What's New** button. You will see a list of highlighted underlined links to Web sites. Click on a link and EXPLORE. HAVE FUN! If you are using Explorer, investigate the Home Page that you are viewing.

3. *Save your favorite pages* by making a bookmark or an addition to your Favorites List.

    When you find a page that you may want to visit at a later time, click on the pull-down menu, **Bookmarks**. Next, click on the menu item **Add Bookmark**. (Explorer—select the **Favorites** menu.)

    Click on the **Bookmarks** (**Favorites**) pull-down menu again. Notice the name of the page you marked listed below the **View Bookmarks**

menu item. To view this page again, select the **Bookmarks** pull-down menu and click on the name of the page you saved.

4. Continue your exploration by clicking on the **What's Cool** button.

5. After you have linked to several pages, click on the **Go** pull-down menu. Notice the listing of the places you have most recently visited. If you want to revisit any of the pages you have already viewed, click on the name of the Web site.

Practice 2:
Organizing and Using Bookmarks

In this practice you will learn how to organize, modify, save, and move bookmark files. If you are using Explorer, save your favorite URLs by using either the **Favorites** button or the **Favorites** menu.

Before you can organize and work with bookmark files, you must access Netscape's **Bookmark** window. There are two ways to access the **Bookmark** window:

- Go to the **Bookmarks** pull-down menu and select **Go To Bookmarks**; or

- Go to the **Window** pull-down menu and select **Bookmarks**.

1. *Organizing your bookmarks*. Before you begin saving bookmarks, it is helpful to consider how to *organize* saved bookmarks. Begin by thinking of categories that your bookmarks might be filed under such as Software, Business, Education, Entertainment, Research, and so forth. For each category make a folder. These are the steps for making your bookmark folders.

a. Go to the **Bookmarks** menu and select **Go To Bookmarks**, or go to the **Window** menu and select **Bookmarks**.

FIGURE 3.3
The Netscape **Bookmarks** window

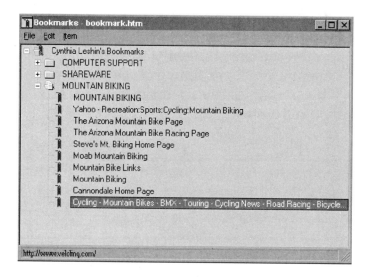

Notice the Web sites saved in the bookmarks folders in Figure 3.3. This Bookmarks window gives you three new menus for working with your bookmarks: **File**, **Edit**, and **Item**.

b. Create a new folder for a bookmark category by selecting the **Item** menu (Fig. 3.4).

FIGURE 3.4
Opened **Item** menu from within the Bookmarks window

c. Select **Insert Folder** (see Fig. 3.5).

FIGURE 3.5
Insert Folder window

d. Type in the name of your folder in the Name dialog box.

e. Enter in a description of the bookmark folder.

f. Click OK.

2. *Adding bookmarks to a folder.* Netscape provides an option for identifying which folder you would like to select to drop your bookmarks in.

a. Select the folder you would like to add your new bookmarks to by clicking on the name of the folder once. The folder should now be highlighted.

b. Go to the **Item** menu and select **Set to New Bookmarks Folder** shown near the bottom of Figure 3.4.

c. Go back to your Bookmark window and notice how this newly identified folder has been marked with a colored bookmark identifier. All bookmarks that you add will be placed in this folder until you identify a new folder.

3. *Modifying the name of your bookmark.* Bookmark properties contain the name of the Web site and the URL. You may want to change the name of the bookmark to indicate more clearly the information available at this site. For example, the bookmark name *STCil/HST Public Information* has very little meaning. Changing its name to *Hubble Space Telescope Public Information* is more helpful later when selecting from many bookmarks.

a. To change the name of a bookmark, select the bookmark by clicking on it once.

b. Go to the **Item** menu from within the Bookmark window.

c. Select **Properties**.

FIGURE 3.6
Properties window from Bookmark **Item** options

Bookmark Properties	✕
General	

Name: The Nine Planets

Location (URL): http://seds.lpl.arizona.edu/nineplanets/nine

Description:

Last Visited: Sat Feb 10 14:49:01 1996

Added on: Sat Feb 10 14:46:20 1996

| OK | Cancel | Apply | Help |

d. Enter in the new name for your bookmark by either deleting the text shown in Figure 3.6 or begin typing the new name when the highlighted text is visible.

e. Notice the URL for the bookmark; you can also enter in a new description for the URL.

4. *Making copies of your bookmarks for adding to other folders.* Occasionally you will want to save a bookmark in several folders. There are two ways to do this:

a. Select the bookmark that you would like to copy. Go to the **Edit** menu from within the Bookmark window and select **Copy**. Select the folder where you would like to place the copy of the bookmark. Go to the **Edit** menu and select **Paste**.

b. Make an alias of your bookmark by selecting **Make Alias** from the **Item** menu. When the alias of your bookmark has been created, move the alias bookmark to the new folder (see "Note").

> ## NOTE
> Bookmarks can be moved from one location to another by dragging an existing bookmark to a new folder.

5. *Deleting a bookmark.* To remove a bookmark:

a. Select the bookmark to be deleted by clicking on it once.

b. Go to the **Edit** menu from within the Bookmark window.

c. Choose either **Cut** or **Delete**.

6. *Exporting and saving bookmarks.* Netscape provides options for making copies of your bookmarks to either save as a backup on your hard drive, to share with others, or to use on another computer.

Follow these steps for exporting or saving your bookmarks to a floppy disk.

a. Open the **Bookmark** window.

b From within the Bookmark window, go to the **File** menu. Select **Save As.**

c. Designate where you would like to save the bookmark file—on your hard drive or to a floppy disk—in the **Save in** box.

FIGURE 3.7
Netscape Bookmark window for saving bookmark files

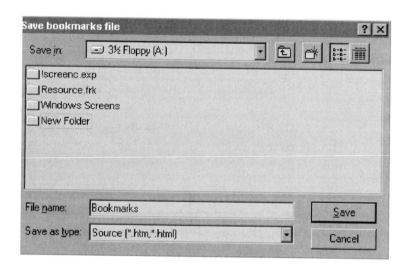

d. Enter in a name for your bookmark file in the **File name** dialog box.

e. Click **Save.**

7. *Importing Bookmarks.* Bookmarks can be imported into Netscape from a previous Netscape session saved on a floppy disk.

a. Insert the floppy disk with the bookmark file into your computer.

b. Open the **Bookmark** window.

c. From within the Bookmark window, go to the **File** menu and select **Import** (see Fig. 3.8).

d. Designate where the bookmark file is located: The **Look in** window displays a floppy disk or you can click on the scroll arrow to bring the hard drive into view.

FIGURE 3.8
Import window allows bookmark files from a floppy disk to be imported into your Netscape application

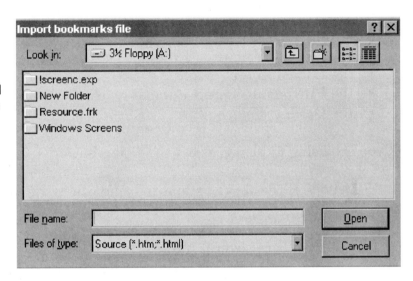

e. Click on **Open**. The bookmarks will now be imported into your Netscape bookmark list.

Practice 3:
Exploring the Internet With Your Web Browser

In this practice you will enter in URL addresses to link to World Wide Web (WWW) sites.

There are three options in Netscape for entering in a URL:

- the **Location** text field;
- the **File** menu—**Open Location;** or
- the **Open** toolbar button.

If you are using Explorer, select the **Open** button.

1. Select one of the above options to bring you to the window where you can enter your choice of URL text.

2. Listed below are several interesting Web sites to visit. Type a URL and EXPLORE. Remember to save your favorite sites as Bookmarks/Favorites.

Awesome List: **http://www.clark.net/pub/journalism/awesome.html**

CityNet: **http://www.city.net**

ESPNetSportsZone: **http://espnet.sportzone.com**

NASA: **http://www.nasa.gov**

Time Warner Pathfinder:
http://www.timeinc.com/pathfinder/Greet.html

The White House: **http://www.whitehouse.gov**

CHAPTER 4
Chatting on the Net

• •

Although the Internet was created as a research network, it soon became popular for chatting and discussing work-related topics and hobbies. In this chapter you will learn how to communicate with others using

➻ listserv mailing lists.
➻ Usenet newsgroups.
➻ Internet Relay Chat (IRC).
➻ Internet phones.

• •

People today are on the Internet because they value and enjoy the interactivity and the relationships they build within the virtual community of cyberspace. The way companies, institutions, and individuals communicate has changed. Internet communication involves five major services: electronic mail, electronic discussion groups (listservs and Usenet), Internet Relay Chat (IRC), Internet phones, and desktop Internet videoconferencing. E-mail and electronic discussion groups are delayed response media. IRC, Net phones, and desktop videoconferencing are real-time media. Net phones and videoconferencing are usually used for private conversations and IRC as a public forum. Electronic mail is most often used for private conversations; electronic discussion groups are used for public conversation.

Listserv Mailing Lists

With so much attention on the World Wide Web, many new Internet users miss learning about electronic mailing lists (also referred to as lists, listservs, or discussion groups) as an Internet resource for finding and sharing information. Electronic mailing lists began in the 1960s when scientists and educators used the Internet to share information and research. Early programs, known as *listservs*, ran on mainframe computers and used e-mail to send reports or studies to a large group of users.

Today, listservs perform the same function—the sharing of information. There are hundreds of special interest lists where individuals can join a virtual community to share and discuss topics of mutual interest.

What Is a Listserv Mailing List?

A *listserv* is the automated system that distributes electronic mail. E-mail is used to participate in electronic mailing lists. Listservs perform two functions:

- distributing text documents stored on them to those who request them, and
- managing interactive mailing lists.

Listservs and text documents

A listserv can be used to distribute information, in the form of text documents, to others. For example, online workshops may make their course materials available through a listserv. The listserv is set up to distribute the materials to participants at designated times. Other examples of documents available through a listserv include: a listing of all available electronic mailing lists, Usenet newsgroups, electronic journals, and books.

Interactive mailing lists

Interactive mailing lists provide a forum where individuals who share interests can exchange ideas and information. Any member of the group may participate in the resulting discussion. This is no longer a one-to-one communication like your e-mail, but rather a one-to-many communication.

Electronic mail written in the form of a report, article, abstract, reaction, or comment is received at a central site and then distributed to the members of the list.

How Does a Mailing List Work?

The mailing list is hosted by a college, university, or institution. The hosting institution uses its computer system to manage the mailing list.

42

Here are a few of the management functions of a listserv:

- receiving requests for subscriptions to the list;
- placing subscribers' e-mail addresses on the list;
- sending out notification that the name has been added to the list;
- receiving messages from subscribers;
- sending messages to all subscribers;
- keeping a record (archive) of activity of the list; and
- sending out information requested by subscribers to the list.

Mailing lists have administrators that may be either a human or a computer program. One function of the administrator is to handle subscription requests. If the administrator is human, you can join the mailing list by communicating in English via an e-mail message. The administrator in turn has the option of either accepting or rejecting your subscription request. Frequently lists administered by a human are available only to a select group of individuals. For example, an executive board of an organization may restrict its list to its members.

Mailing lists administered by computer programs called listservs usually allow all applicants to subscribe to the list. You must communicate with these computer administrators in listserv commands. For the computer administrator to accept your request, you must use the exact format required. The administrative address and how to subscribe should be included in the information provided about a list.

How to Receive Documents From a Listserv

E-mail is used to request text documents distributed by a listserv. The e-mail is addressed to the listserv *administrative address*. In the body of the message a command is written to request the document. The most common command used to request a document is "send" or "get." The command is then followed by the name of the document that you wish to receive. A command to request a list of interesting mailing lists might look like this:

"get" or "send" <name of document>

or

get new-list TOP TEN

How to Join a Listserv Mailing List

To join an interactive mailing list on a topic of interest, send an e-mail message to the list administrator and ask to join the list. Subscribing to an electronic mailing list is like subscribing to a journal or magazine.

- Mail a message to the journal requesting a subscription.

- Include the address of the journal and the address to which the journal will be mailed.

All electronic mailing lists work in the same way.

- E-mail your request to the list administrator at the address assigned by the hosting organization.

- Place your request to participate in the body of your e-mail where you usually write your messages.

- Your return address will accompany your request in the header of your message.

- Your subscription will be acknowledged by the hosting organization or the moderator.

- You will then receive all discussions distributed by the listserv.

- You can send in your own comments and reactions.

- You can unsubscribe (cancel your subscription).

The command to subscribe to a mailing lists looks like this.

<p align="center">**subscribe <name of list> <<em>your name</em>>**
or
subscribe EDUPAGE Cynthia Leshin</p>

The unsubscribe command is similar to the subscribe command.

unsubscribe <name of list> <*your name*>

Active lists may have 50-100 messages from list participants each day. Less active mailing lists may have several messages per week or per month. If you find that you are receiving too much mail or the discussions on the list do not interest you, you can unsubscribe just as easily as you subscribed. If you are going away, you can send a message to the list to hold your mail until further notice.

NOTE

In Chapter 6 you will find the names of several electronic listservs andUsenet newsgroups. Use this list to find listservs and newsgroups of interest to you.

Finding Listserv Mailing Lists

World Wide Web Site for Finding Mailing Lists

Two of the best resources for helping you to find mailing lists are these World Wide Web sites:

> **http://www.liszt.com**
> **http://www.tile.net/tile/listserv/index.html**

E-Mail a Request for Listservs on a Topic

To request information on listserv mailing lists for a particular topic, send an e-mail message to

LISTSERV@vm1.nodak.edu

In the message body type: **LIST GLOBAL /** *keyword*

To find electronic mailing lists you would enter:
LIST GLOBAL/ *business*

Usenet Newsgroups

What Are Newsgroups?

In the virtual community of the Internet, Usenet newsgroups are analogous to a cafe where people with similar interests gather from around the world to interact and exchange ideas. Usenet is a very large, distributed bulletin board system (BBS) that consists of several thousand specialized discussion groups. Currently there are over 20,000 newsgroups with 20 to 30 more added weekly.

You can subscribe to a newsgroup, scan through the messages, read messages of interest, organize the messages, and send in your comments or questions—or start a new one.

Usenet groups are organized by subject and divided into major categories.

Category	Topic Area
alt.	no topic is off limits in this alternative group
comp.	computer-related topics
misc.	miscellaneous topics that don't fit into other categories
news.	happenings on the Internet
rec.	recreational activities/hobbies
sci.	scientific research and associated issues
soc.	social issues and world cultures
talk.	discussions and debates on controversial social issues

In addition to these categories there are local newsgroups with prefixes that indicate their topic or locality.

Some newsgroups are moderated and reserved for very specific articles. Articles submitted to these newsgroups are sent to a central site. If the article is approved, it is posted by the moderator. Many newsgroups have no moderator and there is no easy way to determine whether a group is moderated. The only way to tell if a group is moderated is to submit an article. You will be notified if your article has been mailed to the newsgroup moderator.

What Is the Difference Between Listserv Mailing Lists and Usenet Newsgroups?

One analogy for describing the difference between a listserv mailing list and a Usenet newsgroup is to compare the difference between having a few intimate friends over for dinner and conversation (a listserv) vs. going to a Super Bowl party to which the entire world has been invited (newsgroups). A listserv is a smaller, more intimate place to discuss issues of interest. A Usenet newsgroup is much larger and much more open to "everything and anything goes." This is not to say that both do not provide a place for valuable discussion. However, the size of each makes the experiences very different.

A listserv mailing list is managed by a single site, such as a university. Subscribers to a mailing list are automatically mailed messages that are sent to the mailing list submission address. A listserv would find it difficult to maintain a list for thousands of people.

Usenet consists of many sites that are set up by local Internet providers. When a message is sent to a Usenet site, a copy of the message that has been received is sent to other neighboring, connected Usenet sites. Each of these sites keeps a copy of the message and then forwards the message to other connected systems. Usenet can therefore handle thousands of subscribers.

One advantage of Usenet groups over a mailing list is that you can quickly read postings to the newsgroup. When you connect to a Usenet newsgroup and see a long list of articles, you can select only those that interest you. Unlike a mailing list, Usenet messages do not accumulate in your mailbox, forcing you to read and delete them. Usenet articles are on your local server and can be read at your convenience.

Netscape and Usenet Newsgroups

Netscape supports Usenet newsgroups. You can subscribe to a newsgroup, read articles posted to a group, and reply to articles. You can determine whether your reply is sent to the individual author of the posted article or to the entire newsgroup.

Netscape has an additional feature. Every news article is scanned for references to other documents called URLs. These URLs are shown as active hypertext links that can be accessed by clicking on the underlined words.

Newsgroups have a URL location. These URLs are similar, but not identical, to other pages. For example, the URL for a recreational backcountry newsgroup is **news:rec.backcountry**. The server protocol is **news:** and the newsgroup is **rec.backcountry.**

Newsgroups present articles along what is called a "thread." The thread packages the article with responses to the article. Each new response is indented one level from the original posting. A response to a response is indented another level. Newsgroups' threads, therefore, appear as an outline.

Buttons on each newsgroup page provide the reader with controls for reading and responding to articles. Netscape buttons vary depending on whether you are viewing a page of newsgroup listings or a newsgroup article.

Netscape News Window for Usenet News

To display the News window, go to the **Window** menu and select **Netscape News**.

FIGURE 4.1

The Netscape **News** window

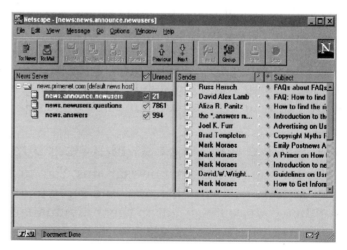

Notice that you have new options in the form of toolbar buttons and pull-down menus for receiving, reading, replying to, and sending messages to newsgroups. Netscape News works in much the same way as Netscape Mail.

Netscape News window buttons

To: News: Displays a Message Composition window for creating a new message posting for a newsgroup.

To: Mail: Displays a Message Composition window for creating a new mail message.

Re: Mail: Click on this button to reply to the current newsgroup message (thread) you are reading.

Re: Both: Displays a Message Composition window for posting a reply to the current message thread for the entire newsgroup and to the sender of the news message.

Forward: Displays the Message Composition window for forwarding the current news message as an attachment. Enter the e-mail address in the **Mail To** field.

Previous: Brings the previous unread message in the thread to your screen.

Next: Brings the next unread message in the thread to your screen.

Thread: Marks the message threads you have read.

Group: Marks all messages read.

Print: Prints the message you are reading.

Stop: Stops the current transmission of messages from your news server.

Netscape News Menus

When you select Netscape News you will receive not only new toolbar buttons but also different pull-down menus for interacting with the Netscape news reader: File, Edit, View, Message, Go, Options, Window, and Help.

> ### NOTE
> This guide does not give detailed information on using Netscape Navigator for Usenet newsgroups. For more information refer to *Netscape Adventures—Step-by-Step Guide to Netscape Navigator and the World Wide Web* by Cynthia Leshin.
>
> For information on using Internet Explorer for newsgroups, see Explorer's online **Help** menu.

Reading Usenet News With Netscape Navigator

Netscape Navigator provides four ways to access newsgroups.

- If you know the name of the newsgroup, type the URL in the location field of the Netscape main menu.

- From within the Netscape News window, go to the **File** menu and select **Add Newsgroup**. Enter the name of the newsgroup in the dialog box.

- From within the Netscape News window, go to the **Options** menu and select **Show All Newsgroups**. From this list, select a newsgroup and check the **Subscribe** box beside the newsgroup name.

- From a World Wide Web site, click on a link to a newsgroup or a newsgroup message.

FIGURE 4.2
Netscape News window
Options menu

Chats

Chats are programs that allow you to talk to many people at the same time from all over the world. Internet Relay Chat (IRC) is the most widely used program and has become one of the most popular Internet services. IRC has produced a new type of virtual community formed mainly by many young people. Although information may be exchanged on any topic and users can send and receive files, the primary use of IRC seems to be more social than business.

Many Internet access providers make IRC available to subscribers. Some institutions have IRC client programs installed. To connect to IRC, users merely type **irc**. If your institution does not have an IRC client program, you can Telnet to a public IRC server and chat from there. Some World Wide Web sites will have chat rooms for interactive discussion on topics of interest. For example, Time Warner's Pathfinder Web site has a chat room for discussing news of the day. Wired magazine has a chat room open for discussion.

After you have connected to an IRC, you will have to choose an online name, known as a *nickname,* to identify yourself. You will be known by your nickname. Next, you select a group or discussion topic, known as a *channel*, to join. There are any number of channels in IRC and any number of people within a channel. Some channels exist all the time; others come and go.

Conversations within chats are text-based. Users type in their message line by line. As a line is being typed, others on the channel see the message. Messages cannot be edited before they are sent to others on the channel. Anyone on the channel can respond to a message as it is revealed on their computer screen by merely typing in their response line by line.

Commercial services such as America Online, CompuServe, Prodigy, and Microsoft Network offer chat rooms for their members to communicate and meet others who have similar interests. Chat rooms with these services can be public or private. Public rooms are created by the service provider and tend to have focused discussion topics. Some of these rooms are hosted, others are not. Some of these chat rooms are available on a regular basis, others are created for special events such as a guest who is online for a forum for several hours.

Private chat rooms are created by members and can hold between 2 and 25 or more registered online users. Private chat rooms may be used for a meeting or just a casual chat between friends. There is no way as to yet see a list of private chat rooms.

If you are interested in learning more about chats, check with your Internet service provider to see if IRC is available, or whether you will need to Telnet to an IRC client server. If you are a member of a commercial online service, check for information on its public and private chat rooms. To experience chat using the World Wide Web, explore these sites.

WebChat Broadcasting System **http://wbs.net**
HotWired **http://www.hotwired.com**
Globe **http://globe1.csuglab.cornell.edu/global/homepage.html**

Internet Phones

The Internet has made possible the global transmission of text, graphics, sound, and video. Now, a new service has come upon the Internet shore making the real-time transmission of voice possible. New products known as Internet phones let you use your computer as a telephone. Internet phones are the hottest new Internet service to talk with another person anywhere in the world at no more than the cost of your local Internet access. Internet telephones can operate over cable, satellite, and other networks.

However, Internet phones are still in their infancy and not yet a substitute for conventional phones. At this stage in their development, they are still a novelty and far from practical to use as a business tool or for routine communication. To reach another person via the Internet phone, both parties need to be running the same software and be online at the same time when the call is made, otherwise the phone won't ring. Currently, most Internet phone software is similar to Internet Relay Chat programs that help users running the same program find and communicate with each other.

Part of the appeal of the Internet phone is the capability to talk to anyone in the world without the cost of a long distance phone call. For the monthly cost of an Internet account two people anywhere in the world can talk for as long and as often as they choose. When one compares this to the cost of national and international phone calls, many are willing to overlook the current limitations and difficulties imposed by this new technology on its users.

The capability and possibilities of the Internet phone have threatened traditional telecommunications companies. The American Carriers Telecommunication Association (ACTA) wants the Federal Communications Commission (FCC) to regulate Internet telephone products. Currently, there are no restrictions on the Net phone, but this could change as hearings are being conducted over the coming months. To keep up to date on these events visit these two Web sites: **http://www.von.org** or **http://www.netguide.com/net**

How Do I Talk to Someone Using an Internet Phone?

There are two ways that you can communicate with Internet users on Net phones:

- through a central server, similar to an Internet Relay Chat server
- connect to a specific individual by using their IP (Internet Protocol) address

Some Internet users have their own IP addresses; others are assigned an IP address every time they log on. Check with your Internet provider for information on your IP address.

What Do I Need to Use an Internet Phone?

Hardware

Before you can chat using Internet phones you will need the following hardware:

- a sound card for your Macintosh or Windows system
- speakers on your computer
- a microphone for your computer

Sound Card

To have a conversation where both parties can speak at the same time, you will need to have a sound card that supports full duplexing. Many Macintosh computers (including the Power Macs) support full-duplex sound. If you are using a PC, check your existing sound card. Full-duplex drivers are available if your sound card does not support full duplexing.

Speakers

The speakers that come with your computer are adequate for the current Net phones. The audio quality of this new technology is not yet what you are accustomed to with traditional telephones.

Microphone

Many computers come with microphones that will be suitable for use with the Internet phones. If you need to purchase a microphone, do not spend more than $10 to $15 on a desktop microphone.

Software

There are several Net phone products that were tested and recommended in the spring of 1996 by *Internet World* magazine:

- VocalTec's Internet Phone
- Quarterdeck Corp's Web Talk
- CoolTalk

Internet Phone (IPhone) was the first Net phone introduced to Internet users in early 1995. After the release and testing of many versions in 1995, the IPhone is considered one of the better Net phones with highly rated sound quality. IPhone is easy to use and resembles the chat environments. When you begin the program you log onto a variety of Internet servers and have the option of joining a discussion group. Once you have joined a group you can call an online user simply by double-clicking on the user's name. This capability is considered to be one of IPhone's strongest points.

The disadvantage of IPhone is that you cannot connect to a specific individual using their IP address. All connections must be made by first connecting to IPhone's IRC-style servers. Both individuals must be online at the same time and connected to the server.

Internet Phone has a free demo version with a one-week trial period. For more information visit their Web site at **http://www.vocaltec.com** or call (201) 768-9400.

Web Talk is the software program of choice for Internet users with their own IP address. To connect to a specific individual, just enter their IP address. The person you are trying to connect with must also be online at the same time. To talk with other online users, connect to WebTalk's server. To learn more about WebTalk visit its Web site at **http://www.webtalk.qdeck.com** or call (301) 309-3700.

CoolTalk is distributed by Netscape Communications Corp. and has a cool feature, the whiteboard, that sets it apart from other Internet phone programs. The whiteboard option becomes available after you have connected to another individual. (Connections are made by either logging onto their global server or entering in an individual's IP address.) The whiteboard begins as a blank window. Using standard paint program tools you can enter text, sketch out ideas, draw, or insert graphics. The whiteboard makes this Net phone a most attractive program for Internet business users.

Netscape 3.0 incorporates CoolTalk into its Navigator software. Download a version by connecting to **http://www.netscape.com** or call (717) 730-9501.

> **NOTE**
>
> Keep an eye on Intel's Internet-Phone. This software is free and has the advantage of allowing users to talk with those using different phone software. MCI has plans to launch a service in partnership with Intel to provide telephone and video services to businesses. **http://www.intel.com**

> **NOTE**
>
> You can also chat across the Internet using videoconferencing programs such as CU-SeeMe. This program makes it possible for interaction with one individual, small groups, or hundreds in a broadcast. Not only do you hear individuals, but you also can see them in full color on your computer monitor. This program has a whiteboard feature for document collaboration.
>
> CU-SeeMe runs on Windows or Macintosh over a 28.8 modem. If you have a 14.4 modem only, audio is possible. To learn more, visit their Web site at **http://www.cu-seeme.com/iw.htm** or call (800) 241-PINE.

CHAPTER 5
Finding Information and
Resources on the Internet

In this chapter, you will learn how to find information and resources on the Internet. You will be using search directories and search engines to find information of interest to you, your career, and your field of study. You will also learn about the following search tools:

- Yahoo (search directory)
- Magellan (search directory)
- Galaxy (search directory)
- Excite (search engine and search directory)
- Alta Vista (search engine)
- Infoseek (search engine and search directory)
- Open Text (search engine)

The Internet contains many tools that speed the search for information and resources. Research tools called "search directories" and "search engines" are extremely helpful.

Search Directories
Search directories are essentially descriptive registries of Web sites. They also have searching options. When you connect to their page, you will find a query box for entering in keywords. The search engine at these sites searches only for keyword matches in the directories' databases. Directories are excellent places to begin your research.

Search Engines
Search engines are different from search directories in that they search World Wide Web sites, Usenet newsgroups, and other Internet resources to find matches to your descriptor keywords. Many search engines also rank the results according to a degree of relevancy. Most search engines provide options for advanced searching to refine your search.

Basic Guidelines for Using a Search Engine

Search directories and search engines are marvelous tools to help you find information on the Internet. Search directories are often the best places to begin a search, as they frequently yield more relevant returns on a topic than a search engine, which may produce a high proportion of irrelevant information. Therefore, it is essential that you use several search tools for your research.

The basic approach to finding information involves the following steps:

1. Use search directories such as Yahoo (**http://www.yahoo.com**), Excite (**http://www.excite.com**), Galaxy (**http://galaxy.einet.net/galaxy.html**), Magellan (**http://magellan.mckinley.com**) or Infoseek (**http://guide.infoseek.com**) to search for the information under a related topic or category. Explore the links that seem relevant to your topic, and make bookmarks of the ones you would like to further investigate. Look for one site that has a large collection of links on your topic. This is the resource goldmine that you are looking for.

2. Use search engines to further research your topic by determining one or more descriptive words (keywords) for the subject. Enter your keywords into the search dialog box.

3. Determine how specific you want your search to be. Do you want it to be broad or narrow? Use available options to refine or limit your search. Some search engines permit the use of boolean operators (phrases or words such as "and," " or," and "not" that restrict a search). Others provide HELP for refining searches, and some have pull-down menus or selections to be checked for options.

4. Submit your query.

5. Review your list of hits (a search return based on a keyword).

6. Adjust your search based on the information returned. Did you receive too much information and need to narrow your search? Did you receive too little or no information and need to broaden your keywords?

Yahoo

Yahoo is one of the most popular search tools on the Internet and is an excellent place to begin your search. Although Yahoo is more accurately described as a search directory, this Web site has an excellent database with search options available. Yahoo can be accessed from the Netscape Search Directory button, or by entering this URL: **http://www.yahoo.com**

There are two ways to find information using Yahoo: search through the subject index, or use the built-in search engine.

Yahoo Subject Index

When you connect to Yahoo, you will see a list of subjects or directories. Select the topic area that best fits your search needs. Follow the links until you find the information you are searching for.

Using Yahoo to Search for Information

Follow these steps to use Yahoo to search for information:

1. Begin by browsing the subject directory. For example, if you were searching for information on "how businesses use the Internet to communicate with customers," you would first select the *Business and Economy* directory and then follow the links to *Companies*. Explore, and see how companies are using the Internet to provide interactive communication services.

2. Yahoo's search engine can also be used to find information. Enter a descriptive keyword for your subject, one that uniquely identifies or describes what you are looking for. It is often helpful to do a broad search first, though results often provide information on the need to change descriptive keywords or to refine your query.

   Perhaps you know the name of a company, such as Silicon Graphics, that takes advantage of the Internet as an interactive medium to provide entertaining consumer content and services. Enter the name of the company, in this case "Silicon Graphics" (see Fig. 5.1).

3. Click on the **Search** button and review your query results (see Fig. 5.2).

FIGURE 5.1

Yahoo search form and subject index in which the keywords "Silicon Graphics" have been entered

FIGURE 5.2

Yahoo search results from the keywords "Silicon Graphics"

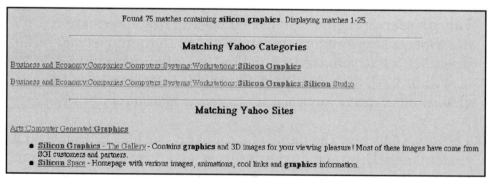

4. You may now want to refine your search. Most search engines have options for advanced searching using boolean logic or more carefully constructed database queries. Review the search page for **Options** or **Advanced Options**. When using Yahoo, click on the **Options** button.

   If you are using two keywords, do you want Yahoo to look for either word (boolean **or**), both keywords (boolean **and**), or all words as a single string? For example, in the search for "business communication" select boolean **and** because you want to find resources that contain both words "business" **and** "communication" in their titles (see Fig. 5.3). Otherwise the search would be too broad and would find all resources that contained either of the keywords "business" **or** "communication."

FIGURE 5.3
Yahoo **Options** for refining a search

Find all listings containing the *keys*(separated by space)
business communication [Search] [Clear]
Search ◉ Yahoo! ◯ Usenet ◯ Email Addresses
Find only new listings added during the past [3 years]
Find listings that contain
◯ At least one of the *keys*(boolean **or**)
◉ All *keys*(boolean **and**)
Consider *keys* to be
◯ Substrings
◉ Complete words
Display [25] listings per page

5. Further limit or expand your search by selecting Substrings or Complete words. For example, with your *business communication* search, you would select the search option for *Complete words,* or Yahoo treats the word as a series of letters rather than a whole word. A research return using substrings would include all incidences where both the words *business* and *communication* appeared in any form.

6. Determine the number of matches you want returned for your search.

7. Submit your query.

8. Review your return list of hits and adjust your search again if necessary.

9. Review your return list for other descriptive words that have been used when summarizing search results. For example, when using keywords "business communication," search result summaries produced other important descriptive words such as "Internet communication" and "computer-mediated communication."

10. Conduct a search using other descriptive words.

Magellan and Galaxy

Magellan (**http://magellan.mckinley.com**) and Galaxy (**http://galaxy.einet.net/galaxy.html**) are two other excellent search directories. Magellan provides options for narrowing or expanding your search by selecting sites rated from one to four stars (four stars being the most restricted). You can also exclude sites with mature content by restricting your search to "Green Light" sites only (a green light will be displayed next to the review).

FIGURE 5.4
Home page for Magellan with options for specializing your search

Excite

Excite provides the fullest range of services of all the search tools. Excite searches scanned Web pages and Usenet newsgroups for keyword matches and creates summaries of each match. Excite also has a Web directory organized by category. Excite consists of three services:

- **NetSearch**—comprehensive and detailed searches

- **NetReviews**—organized browsing of the Internet, with site evaluations and recommendations

- **Excite** Bulletin—an online newspaper with reviews of Internet resources, a newswire service from Reuters, and its own Net-related columns

Excite offers two different types of search options: concept-based searching and keyword searching. The search engines described thus far have used keyword search options. Keyword searches are somewhat limited due to the necessity of using boolean qualifiers.

Concept-based searching goes one step beyond keyword searches—finding what you mean and not what you say. Using the phrase "communicating with media," a concept-based search will find documents that most closely match this phrase. Excite is available at **http://www.excite.com**

Searching With Excite

1. Type in a phrase that fits your information need. Be as specific as you can, using words that uniquely relate to the information you are looking for, not simply general descriptive words. For example, for your media communication search enter the following phrase: *communicating with media*

FIGURE 5.5
Excite Web page displaying concept-based search
using the phrase *communicating with media*

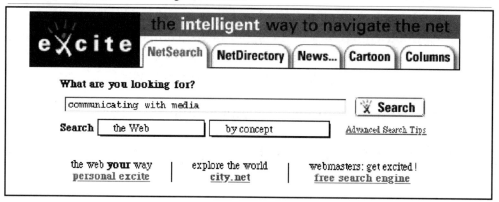

2. If the search result does not contain the information you are looking for, or if the returns provide too much irrevelant information, use the Advanced Search options.

3. Advanced features include the use of a plus sign (**+**) in front of a search word to ensure that all the returns contain that word. Use a minus sign (**-**) in front of a search word and Excite will make sure that NO documents contain the word. Excite also supports the use of boolean operators (**AND**, **OR**, **NOT**).

4. Excite lists 10 search results at a time in decreasing order of confidence. Each result lists a title, a URL, and a brief summary of the document. The percentage to the left of the return is the confidence rating (Figure 5.7), with 100% being the highest confidence rating attainable. To see the next listing of documents related to your phrase or keywords, click the "next documents" button. Click the "sort by site" button to view the Web sites that have the most pages relevant to your search.

FIGURE 5.6

Search results for *communicating with media*
(concept-based search) with a percentage
of confidence rating for finding relevant information

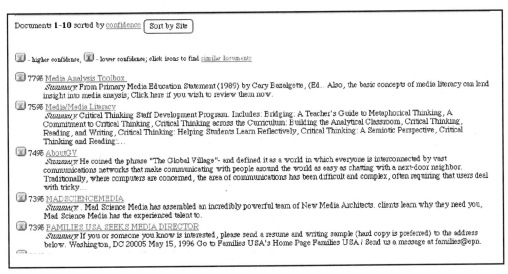

FIGURE 5.7

Excite search showing
percentage of
confidence rating

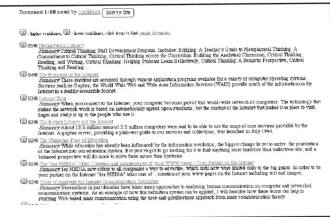

Alta Vista

Digital's Alta Vista is considered one of the best search engines currently
available, with one of the largest Web-search databases. Alta Vista's
searches are consistently more comprehensive than any of the other search
tools. Although you will spend a great deal of time browsing your search

results, you will be provided with as much information as possible on a search query. **http://altavista.digital.com**

Use Alta Vista to search for information on "interactive advertising." Conduct two searches: a simple query and an advanced query.

1. A simply query is conducted by entering in keywords or phrases. Do not use AND or OR to combine words when doing a simple query. For this query, type in the phrase: *interactive advertising*

FIGURE 5.8
Alta Vista Home Page

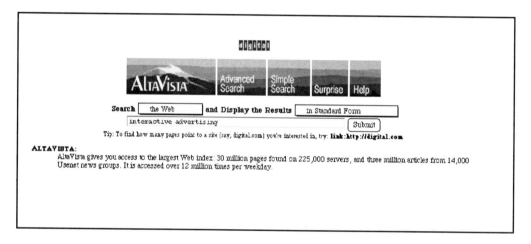

2. Alta Vista's advanced options use the binary operators AND, OR, and NEAR and the operator NOT. For more information on the advanced options, click on the *Help for Advanced Options*.

Conduct a more refined search using Alta Vista's advanced options, enter the following words: *interactive AND advertising AND Internet.*

FIGURE 5.9

Alta Vista advanced options search using the binary operator AND

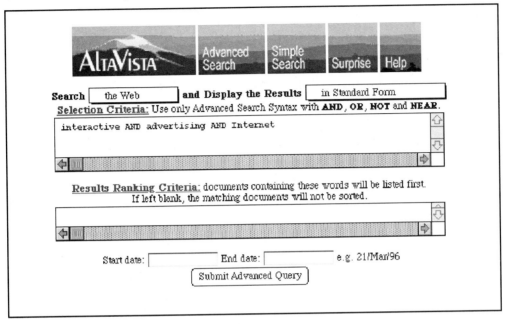

Infoseek is a professional service provided by Infoseek Corporation. In 1995, Infoseek introduced its easy-to-use search services to subscribers for a monthly subscription fee. Because of its popularity, the services have been expanded to include two new options: Infoseek Guide and Infoseek Professional.

Infoseek Guide is the free service that integrates the latest search technology with a browsable directory of Internet resources located on World Wide Web sites, Usenet newsgroups, and other popular Internet resource sites. Users can choose to use the search engine and enter keywords or phrases, or browse the navigational directories.

Visit the InfoSeek Guide site and try these tools for finding Internet information and resources. **http://guide.infoseek.com**

Infoseek Professional is a subscription-based service that offers individuals and business professionals comprehensive access to many Internet resources such as newswires, publications, broadcast programs, business, medical, financial, and government databases. The difference between Infoseek Guide and Professional is the capability to conduct more comprehensive searches and to have options for refining and limiting searches. For example, you can conduct a search query by just entering in a question such as "How are companies using the Internet for communication with customers?" You can also limit your query to just the important words or phrases that are likely to appear in the documents you are looking for:

"communicating" with "customers" using the "Internet"

By identifying the key words or phrases (**communicating, customers**, and **Internet**) with quotes, your search accuracy is greatly enhanced.

Infoseek Professional offers a free trial period. To learn how to perform the most efficient search, link to Infoseek's information on search queries and examples. **http://professional.infoseek.com**

FIGURE 5.10
Infoseek guide for information and resources

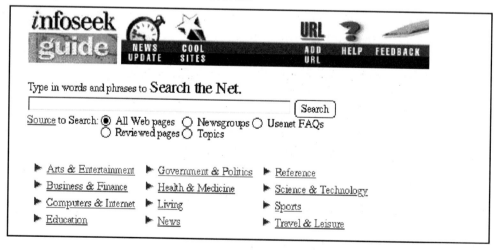

Open Text

Open Text has one of the most comprehensive collections of search tools and is one of the best designed search engines on the Internet.
http://www.opentext.com

Open Text offers many search options:

- simple query on words;
- a power search using up to five operators between terms (*and, or, not, but not, near,* and *followed by*);
- options to create your own weighted search;
- results scored by relevancy; and
- an option to show a report of where Open Text found your search matches.

Open Text produces better returns on your search if you break up a phrase into keywords. For example, when "using the Internet to communicate with customers" was entered, Open Text reported many irrelevant results. When the query was changed to the individual search terms, "business" "communication" and "media," a large number of relevant results was displayed.

FIGURE 5.11
Open Text page showing query entered with
three search terms: "business" "communication" "media"

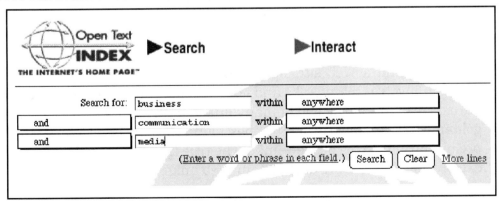

Search Guidelines—The Treasure Hunt

- Begin your search by looking for relevant documents in search directories such as Yahoo, Excite, Galaxy, Magellan, and Infoseek.

- Use search engines to further your search. Using descriptive keywords, run a search. Preliminary searches provide you with an overview of what is available on your topic and how effective your search was in finding the information you are looking for.

- Use the results of these preliminary searches to refine your search. Review results for other descriptive words that have been used in search summaries.

- Check for advanced search options in the search engine you are using. Some may offer options using boolean qualifiers such as AND or OR to limit your search. Others may have you enter a (+) sign in front of all words that must be included in the search.

- Use more than one search engine. You will find that search results vary depending on which search tool you use.

- Think of related or associated places that might have information on your topic. For example, in researching the Olympics, in addition to a search using the keyword "Olympics," you might research the name of the city where the Olympic games are to be held, the station televising the games, and other news or sports channels with Web sites such as ESPN. Your search engine(s) may not find the best Web sites from the television or news stations.

- When you find a Web site, spend time exploring the links. Internet research involves many links and going deeper into them. You will find buried treasures at the end of many linked pathways. The information goldmines are frequently not the ones found by your search engine or by preliminary checking of a few links. The true treasures come from much exploration and digging deep within Web links.

PART II

The Web and Business Communication

CHAPTER 6
Cool Business Communication Web Sites

In this chapter, you will find many Internet resources to explore and help you discover how the Internet is being used as a communication tool for business. Categories include:

- Cool Business Web Sites
- Business Communication Resources
- Business Resources—General
- Companies—Using Internet Communication Tools
- Companies—Links to Businesses on the Net
- Using the Internet as a Communication Tool
- News—Business
- Speeches and Speech Writing
- Writing Resources
- Business Listserv Mailing Lists
- Business Usenet Newsgroups

Cool Business Web Sites

Many of the sites listed below have been given awards for excellence in content, design, and presentation.

Digital Planet
http://www.digiplanet.com/index.html
For anyone who wants to communicate a message, the most important issue is engaging and retaining one's audience. Whether conveying a corporate message or providing entertaining consumer content, interactive productions must provide compelling and fresh substance to succeed. Digital Planet is a company dedicated to expanding the

interactive medium's power to communicate a message that is entertaining, enlightening, and informative. Since its creation in October of 1994, Digital Planet has continually broken new ground in exploring creative ways to bring meaning and importance to Web sites for their corporate clients, advertisers, and consumers. This company is among the leaders creatively shaping the interactive media of tomorrow. Visit this site and explore links to learn how the Internet is being used to communicate with customers.

Elements of Style
http://www.columbia.edu/acis/bartleby/strunk
The Elements of Style by William Strunk is a book intended for use in English courses in which the practice of composition is combined with the study of literature.

HOT HOT HOT
http://www.hot.presence.com
Hot Hot Hot is one of the Net's coolest hot sauce shops! A business that has learned how to use the Internet. Visit this site and learn more.

Internet Plaza
http://plaza.xor.com
The Internet Plaza is an excellent place to begin when exploring online commerce. The Internet Plaza brings together exceptional Web sites for you to browse and enjoy. Explore virtual streets or proceed to the PlazaTown for an overview of everything the site has to offer.

Kitty Locker's Introduction to the Web
http://www.cohums.ohio-state.edu/english/facstf/kol/kolhome.htm
This page helps students in business and technical communication classes at The Ohio State University learn to use the Web, do research on the Web, or design home pages.

Speech Writing
http://speeches.com/index.shtml
This award winning site has excellent resources for writing speeches. You're just a click away from everything you need to help you in your

speech preparation. There's a speech archive; links to thousands of other speeches on the Web, free help with your speech writing, and the one and only Automatic Wedding Speech Writer.

Superquotes
http://www.columbia.edu/acis/bartleby/bartlett

Bartlett's familiar quotations, passages, phrases, proverbs traced to their sources.

Tripod
http://www.tripod.com/tripod

Tripod was founded by recent graduates who realized, while they were still in college, that they were unprepared to enter the "real world." They started Tripod to provide the "tools for life" lacking in a traditional education yet necessary to succeed in a changing world—a world where the rules aren't always clear.

At the Tripod site you can build an online résumé with Résumé Doctor, contact your members of Congress through Political Playbook, build your own Home Page with Home Page Builder, or plan your coming year with Reminder Minder. You will also find articles, interviews, and reviews.

Writing Page
http://www.stetson.edu/~hansen/writguid.html

This page is designed to supply as much information and resources as possible for writers. While this site has all types of links, its main focus is helping college students improve their writing skills. This page is a companion page to the Write Your Way to a High GPA page.

Zima Clearmalt
http://www.zima.com/zimag.html

This site is an excellent example of how a business can use entertainment to entice visitors. Zima Clearmalt is a product of Coors Brewing Company. Find out who or what Zima is; join the Zima Fan Club (Tribe Z) or check out the story.

Business Communication Resources

Association for Business Communication Consultants
http://www.iupui.edu/%7Ekdavis/abccc/home.htm
Association For Business Communication Consultants serves as a resource center for people interested in consulting.

Business Communications World Wide Web Resource Center
http://galaxy.einet.net:80/galaxy/Business-and-Commerce/ Management/Communications/lance-cohen.html
Every time you write a purchase order, send an e-mail message, submit an activities report, or express your sympathies to a customer you are using business communication. Many of us take these communications for granted. We allow them to slide by the wayside while we focus on the important things: inventory, cash flow, product, and sale. The royal road to the customer, however, lies along the information superhighway of business communication. Visit this site and investigate how business communication can help develop relationships and build businesses.

Business Language Update
http://www.interlog.com/%7Eflebo/instref.htm
A guide to modern business language.

Business Writing
http://www.interlog.com/~ohi/www/biz.html
Visit the World Wide Web Virtual Library for links to information that will help you to polish your business writing skills.

Business Writing
http://mustang.fste.ac.cowan.edu.au/AAECP/writ_ski/writ_ski.htm
Many excellent resources for helping you to write various business items: general report writing; business correspondence; proposals and tenders; feasibility study; job applications; meetings; media (media releases); committees and boards; packaging and presentation of reports, and much more.

Communications
http://www.smartbiz.com/sbs/cats/comm.htm

This Web site has links to many communication resources: business writing, telephone systems, employee communications, e-mail, presentations, mobile office, facsimiles, and much more.

Editorial Eye
http://www.eei-alex.com/eye

The Eye is a resource for writers, editors, designers, project managers, communications specialists, and everyone else who cares about excellence in publishing practices. Any aspect of effective written communication is likely to appear as a topic in the Eye.

Grammar and Style Notes
http://www.english.upenn.edu/~jlynch/grammar.html

This award winning Web site has articles on grammatical rules and explanations, and comments on style.

Information, Security, and Privacy in Network Environments
http://lucien.sims.berkeley.edu/OTA/info.security/info.security.rpt.txt

Information networks are changing the way we do business, educate our children, deliver government services, and dispense health care. This site has a report that was prepared in response to a request by the Senate Committee on Governmental Affairs and the House Subcommittee on Telecommunications and Finance. The report focuses on policy issues related to Internet communication.

Madalyn
http://www.udel.edu/alex/mba/main/netdir2.html

Madalyn is an excellent business research tool made available by the University of Delaware MBA program. Visit this site to explore links to: accounting, corporate info, economics, entrepreneurship, ethics, finance, international business, management, marketing, quality, and much more.

Speech Writing
http://speeches.com/index.shtml

This award winning site has excellent resources for writing speeches.

You're just a click away from everything you need to help you in your speech preparation. There's a speech archive: links to thousands of other speeches on the Web, free help with your speech writing, and the one and only Automatic Wedding Speech Writer.

Telecommunications Act of 1996
http://www.technologylaw.com/techlaw/act.html
Learn more about the Telecommunications Act passed in 1996. Become more informed on its impact for business and communication.

Visual Presentation Assistant
http://www.ukans.edu/cwis/units/coms2/vpa/vpa.htm
An online tutorial for improving public speaking skills.

Words of Mouth
http://www.cohums.ohio-state.edu/english/facstf/kol/diverse.htm
The Words of Mouth Home Page has been created to meet two distinct needs of editors and others interested in learning more about communication skills.

Business Resources—General

Airlines on the Web
http://haas.berkeley.edu/~seidel/airline.html
"Hello all. Welcome to the Airlines of the WEB page. I am a graduate student at UC Berkeley's Haas School of Business studying the airline industry for my dissertation...." Visit this award-winning site of Marc-David Seidel.

AT&T Business Network
http://www.bnet.att.com
This MUST VISIT site has links to many of the best busines sites on the Web as well as the latest business news and information.

Business Resources on the Internet
gopher://gopher.tamu.edu/11/.dir/business.dir
This Gopher site has information and many links to business resources on the Internet.

CNN Interactive
http://www.cnn.com
This excellent site has links to U.S. news, world news, business, weather, sports, politics, technology, and much more—including search options.

Cultural Diversity
http://www.cohums.ohio-state.edu/english/facstf/kol/diverse.htm
Links to cultural diversity resources on the Internet.

Entrepreneurial Edge Online
http://www.edgeonline.com
Visit this site to learn more about growing your business online.

Federal Express
http://www.fedex.com
FedEx provides a unique service from its site—tracking a FedEx package.

Galaxy
http://galaxy.einet.net/galaxy/Business-and-Commerce/Business-General-Resources.html
This search directory has links to business resources.

Glossary of Business Terms
http://cnnfn.com/resources/glossary/index.html
An excellent resource for finding the definition of business terms.

Hoover's Corporate Directory
http://cnnfn.com/resources/hoover/index.html
Search Hoover's Corporate Directory of over 10,000 public and private companies. Hoover's MasterList Plus provides brief corporate profiles and links to company web presences and other public information.

Interesting Business Sites on the Web
http://www.owi.com/netvalue/v1i1l1.html
Since its inception, the *Interesting Business Sites on the Web* page has listed over 220 innovative and interesting sites for those interested in

business on the Net. Sites included are not just "glitz," but appear to provide significant business value.

iWorld's Guide To Electronic Commerce
http://e-comm.iworld.com
This Web site provides a list of links to sites designed to enhance commerce and trade using the instantaneous capability of online communications, from small business promotions or exploring online banking to corporate advertising and sources on government regulations.

MCI
http://www.internetmci.com
This site was voted as one of the top business sites.

Relais & Chateaux
http://www.integra.fr/relaischateaux
A well-done Web site that provides links to worldwide resorts.

Silicon Graphics
http://www.sgi.com
Surf this excellent site for a look at Silicon Graphics products, services, and entertainment.

Sony
http://www.sony.com
The Sony site is an excellent example of how interactivity can be used on the Internet. It contains links to music, film, and electronics. Information can be found on musicians, their tour schedules, sound clips, record cover art, music videos, and special promotions, as well as information on Sony products.

Southwest Airlines
http://www.iflyswa.com
Visit Southwest Airlines' Home Gate for an example of interactive graphics.

United Parcel Service
http://www.ups.com

Learn more about how businesses provide useful services by visiting the United Parcel Service's interactive site. This site also helps track packages, calculate approximate costs for sending a package, and estimate how long it will take for a package to reach its destination.

Financial Services

Fidelity Investment
http://www.fid-inv.com

Fidelity was one of the first financial services to establish a Web site believing that, given the right tools, individuals make their own best investment decisions. This World Wide Web server provides investors with information and assistance to make more informed choices. It challenges visitors to find out how their personalities impact their ability to save. They can also check out how others scored on the same questions. The site also includes a contest and games.

Bank of America
http://www.bankamerica.com

Buttons on this site offer users the opportunity to learn more about Bank of America, commercial services, personal finance, and community and capital markets.

Publishing

Hot Wired
http://www.hotwired.com

Visit this excellent hypermedia storefront that contains services, advertising, opportunities for advertising, special guest appearances, chat rooms, and much more. This site is an excellent example of the Internet's capabilities to deliver services and products.

New York Times
http://nytimesfax.com/index.html or http://www.nytimes.com

This site delivers highlights from the daily newspaper as well as articles on technology. You will need to download a copy of Adobe Acrobat reader (free) before you can read the nytimesfax online newspaper.

NewsPage
http://www.newspage.com

NewsPage is one of the Web's leading sources of daily business news, with thousands of categorized news stories updated daily.

The San Jose Mercury News
http://www.sjmercury.com/main.htm

The Mercury Center Web is the first complete daily newspaper on the World Wide Web. This service offers continually updated news coverage, the complete text of each day's final edition of *The San Jose Mercury News*, including classified ads, and a variety of special features.

Time Warner
http://www.pathfinder.com

Pathfinder from Time Warner is an excellent Web site for discovering how an information-providing company pushes the capabilities of the new Internet medium.

Voyager
http://www.voyagerco.com

Voyager publishes some of the best laserdiscs and CDs. Visit this site to see a creative design using hypermedia.

Wall Street Journal
http://www.wsj.com

This online version of *The Wall Street Journal* has hyperlinks to money and investing updates, a variety of *Journal* offerings including headlines from today's paper, and *The Wall Street Journal* Classroom Edition—the *Journal's* award-winning educational program for secondary-school students and teachers.

Companies—Using Internet Communication Tools

Business Communication Directory-Newfoundland
http://www.compusult.nf.ca:80/nfld/directory/communic.html

This is a listing of businesses in Newfoundland and Labrador specializing in communication and public relations services.

Coles-Dunford-Kimbell
http://www.cdk.com/cdk

Tell the World! You have a message—maybe it's a good idea, a good product, a good cause, or something everybody ought to know. Let CDK help you tell it with sharp writing and eye-grabbing visuals to create a variety of communication tools, including printed materials such as brochures, newsletters, flyers, and display advertising. Visit this site to learn how one company uses Internet communication tools for providing services to customers.

Communication Strategies
http://www.cstrategies.com

This business site is an excellent example of a small business that provides useful and interesting content or—SERVICE before PRODUCT. Here you will find many interesting links to business resources.

The LIST
http://www.sirius.com/~bam/jul.html

Links to businesses online.

Sun Microsystems
http://www.sun.com

Visit this Web site to learn more about a company that has focused on the convergence of the computer and communication industries.

Targeted Communication Management (TCM)
http://iconode.ca/aim/svc2.html

Targeted Communication Management (TCM) offers a range of services to support communication, consultation, and marketing programs. The TCM approach is to emphasize common sense, cost-effective solutions to business communication requirements.

Companies—Links to Businesses on the Net

Commercial Sites Index
http://www.directory.net
The Commercial Sites Index lists businesses that have set up home pages on the Web. Make this a scheduled visit to see how companies are using the Net for business.

Interesting Business Sites on the Web
http://www.owi.com/netvalue/index.html
This is a relatively small list of sites (less than 50) that covers most of the exciting business uses of the Web. The list is updated frequently, adding new and interesting sites while deleting others.

Internet Business Connection
http://www.charm.net/~ibc
An electronic storefront where you can browse for products and services through an alphabetical listing or by category.

The LIST
http://www.sirius.com/~bam/jul.html
Links to businesses online.

PR NEWSWIRE
http://www.prnewswire.com/cnoc/links.html
http://www.prnewswire.com
PR Newswire has links to what it feels are some of the best and most important business sites.

The 25 Best Business Web Sites
http://techweb.cmp.com:2090/techweb/ia/13issue/13topsites.html
Twenty-five business Web sites have been deemed the "best of the best." Each illustrates at least one of the more sophisticated uses of the Web, and they all have one thing in common—they do on the Web what they couldn't have accomplished in another medium.

News—Business

CNN Financial Network
http://cnnfn.com/index.html
Links to business news include information on managing your money, managing your business, and local and international business news.

Interactive Age Digital
http://www.conceptone.com/netnews/netnews.htm
The online newspaper for electronic commerce.

Internet News Database
http://www.conceptone.com/netnews/netnews.htm
The Internet News Database is a free indexing and abstracting service for the Internet community. The mainstream media and trade magazines are monitored daily for news related to the Internet and commercial online services. The news is condensed into succinct summaries to give online entrepreneurs and marketers quick access to the information that most concerns them.

Madlyn— University of Deleware MBA Program
http://www.udel.edu/alex/mba/main/netdir2.html
Visit this site for links to current business news.

PointCast
http://www.pointcast.com
PointCast Incorporated was founded in 1992 to provide current news and information to anyone on the Internet. The PointCast Network broadcasts personalized news, stock quotes, weather, sports, and more directly to your computer screen.PointCast is one of the HOTTEST new Internet applications.

Using the Internet as a Communication Tool

Analysis for Internet Communication
http://shum.huji.ac.il/jcmc/vol1/issue4/december.html
This very interesting site provides a thought-provoking discussion and analysis on using the Internet for communication.

The Business of the Internet
http://www.rtd.com/people/rawn/business.html

An introduction to the Internet for commercial organizations with a focus on what the Internet can do for businesses: product analysis, market analysis, expert advice and help, recruitment of new employees, rapid information access, wide-scale information dissemination, rapid communication, cost-effective document transfer, peer communication, and new business opportunities.

Future of Interactive Advertising—The Herring Interview
http://www.herring.com/mag/issue13/future.html

When THE HERRING was first considered for digging into the interactive advertising world, its management thought that it was too early in the game to be interesting. Then they read a rather bold comment made by Intel's vice president for corporate development, Avram Miller: "Advertising is probably going to be the killer app for the information highway." Visit this site to learn more about interactive advertising.

Global Village Communication
http://www.info.globalvillag.com/index.html#NewsStand

Global Village develops and markets communication products and services for personal computer users. Visit the different areas in The Village to learn more about communicating from your computer, including faxing, accessing online services and the Internet, and connecting to remote networks.

The Internet, A Revolution in Communication
http://www.nih.gov:80/dcrt/expo/talks/overview/index.html

This site has information on the Internet as a communication medium and links to information on the Internet revolution as reported in the media.

Internet Business Applications Guide
http://www.alter.net/busguide.htm

This site has links to a business guide for using the Internet to achieve a competitive business advantage.

Internet Resources for Technical Communicators
http://www.rpi.edu:80/~perezc2/tc

This page provides a number of links to resources on the Internet that may be of interest to technical communicators. These resources can be used as tools for the improvement of your communication skills since you have the opportunity to share information with other technical communicators around the world. Resources are categorized into electronic mailing lists; newsgroups; electronic journals, newsletters, and magazines; and online dictionaries.

Speeches and Speech Writing

How to Write Your Speech
http://www.coffingco.com/doc/tjwrite.html

Tips for writing a speech for a particular audience.

Public Speaking Anxiety
http://www.mwc.edu/~bchirico/psanxinf.html

Symptoms of public speaking anxiety (PSA) and how to overcome PSA.

Speech Writing
http://speeches.com/index.shtml

This award-winning site has excellent resources for writing speeches. You're just a click away from everything you need to help you in your speech preparation. There's a speech archive: links to thousands of other speeches on the Web, free help with your speech writing, and the one and only Automatic Wedding Speech Writer.

Spin Doctor's Clinic
http://speeches.com/writer.html

Help with your speech draft from the Spin Doctor.

Writing

Business Writing
http://mustang.fste.ac.cowan.edu.au/AAECP/writ_ski/writ_ski.htm

Many excellent resources for helping you to write various business items:

general report writing; business correspondence; proposals and tenders; feasibility study; job applications; meetings; media (media releases); committees and boards; packaging and presentation of reports, and much more.

Business Writing
http://www.interlog.com/~ohi/www/biz.html
Visit the World Wide Web Virtual Library for links to information to help you polish your business writing skills.

Copyright Information for Writers
http://www.inkspot.com/~ohi/inkspot/copyright.html
Information on copyrights and copyrighting.

Editorial Eye
http://www.eei-alex.com/eye
The Eye is a resource for writers, editors, designers, project managers, communications specialists, and everyone else who cares about excellence in publishing practices. Any aspect of effective written communication is likely to appear as a topic in the Eye.

Elements of Style
http://www.columbia.edu/acis/bartleby/strunk
The Elements of Style by William Strunk is a book intended for use in English courses in which the practice of composition is combined with the study of literature.

MLA Style Sheet For Documenting Online Resources
http://www.cas.usf.edu/english/walker/mla.html
Information on how to document online research.

Online Reference Works
http://www.cs.cmu.edu/Web/references.html
This site has a collection of online reference works such as English, foreign and computing dictionaries, acronym guides, thesauri, quotation resources, encyclopedias, and more.

University Writing Resources
http://www.interlog.com/~ohi/inkspot/university.html
Links to many writing resources.

Writer's Block
http://www.magi.com/~niva/writblok/index.html
Writer's Block is a quarterly newsletter that deals with technical writing and the business of documentation. It contains material of interest to communications specialists, including writers, editors, graphic designers, and desktop publishing operators.

Writing Page
http://www.stetson.edu/~hansen/writguid.html
This page is designed to provide as much information and resources as possible for writers. While this site has all types of resources and links, its main focus is helping college students improve their writing skills. This page is a companion page to the Write Your Way to a High GPA page.

Writer's Resource Center
http://www.azstarnet.com/~poewar/writer/writer.html
John Hewitt is the writer and curator of the Writer's Resource Center. Here you will find links to writing tips such as 14 Tips for Sending Effective Press Releases; How to Become an Expert Writer in Any Industry; Technical Writing: Books and Reference Sources; The Art of Networking, and much more.

Writing Resources
http://www.public.iastate.edu/~psisler/resources.html
Writing resources from the University of Iowa for writing instructors, professional communicators, technical writers, and rhetoric and composition scholars.

Writing Resources on the Net
http://owl.trc.purdue.edu/resources.html
Purdue University has compiled many excellent writing resources on the Internet. If you're looking for good indexes and directories, also check out their extensive collection of Writing Labs on the Internet.

Business Listserv Mailing Lists

Communicate with others in the business communication community by subscribing to listserv mailing lists on topics of interest.

Important Information Before You Begin

Mailing lists have two different addresses.

1. An *administrative address* that you will use when you

    *   subscribe to the list.
    *   unsubscribe from the list.
    *   request information or help.

2. A *submission address* used to send your messages to the list.

The Administrative Mail Address

Most listserv mailing lists use software such as listserv, majordomo, or listproc that automatically processes users' requests to subscribe or unsubscribe. Some examples of administrative addresses used for subscribing and unsubscribing are:

> **listserv@uga.cc.uga.edu**
> **majordomo@gsn.org**
> **listproc@educom.unc.edu**

NOTE

Requests for subscriptions are usually processed by computers, therefore type the commands without any changes. Be sure to enter the exact address that you have received, duplicating spacing and upper and lowercase letters. Do not add any other information in the body of your message. If your e-mail package adds a signature, be sure to take it off before sending your request.

After you join a listserv mailing list, you will usually receive notification of your subscription request and an electronic welcome. This message will provide you with information such as the purpose of the list, the names of the listserv's owners, how to subscribe and unsubscribe, and other commands to use for the list.

NOTE

Save a copy of this listserv welcome message. Later you may want to refer to it for information on how to unsubscribe or perform other operations related to the list.

The Submission Mail Address

Mail sent to the submission address is read by all of the subscribers to the list. This address will be different and should not be used for communicating with the list administrator. Here is an example of an address for sending your messages to the mailing list participants:

itforum@uga.cc.uga.edu

For this mailing list, the first word is the name of the list, *itforum* (instructional technology forum). Any mail sent to this address will be sent to all subscribers to the list. This is the address used to communicate with subscribers to the list.

• •

Subscribing To A Listserv Mailing List

In this section you will find business communication listserv mailing lists. You will be given the address to which to send your request and the subscription request format for the BODY of your message. Leave the SUBJECT field blank. If your e-mail program requires you to make an entry in the SUBJECT field, insert a period (.).

The format for each listserv will be the same as in the example (Fig. 6.1).

> Address: listserv@kentvm.kent.edu
> Subject: leave blank
> Body: subscribe ADDICT-L <firstname lastname>

FIGURE 6.1
Subscription to a listserv

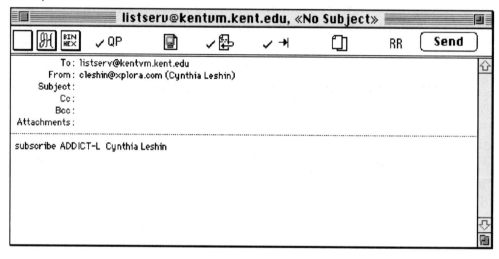

BizCom (Business Communication Research, Pedagogy, and Practice)
Address: listproc@ebbs.english.vt.edu
Body: subscribe BizCom <firstname lastname>

BSN-D (Business Sources on the Net—Distribution List)
Address: listserv@listserv.kent.edu
Body: sub BSN-D <firstname lastname>

BTECH94 (Business Technology)
Address: listserv@umslvma.umsl.edu
Body: sub BTECH94 <firstname lastname>

BUSETH-L (Business Ethics Computer Network)
Address: listserv@ubvm.cc.buffalo.edu
Body: sub BUSETH-L <firstname lastname>

CMC (Computer Mediated Communication)
Address: listserv@vm.its.rpi.edu
Body: sub CMC <firstname lastname>

COMHIST (History of Human Communication)
Address: listserv@vm.its.rpi.edu
Body: sub COMHIST <firstname lastname>

INBUSINESS (Internet in Business Discussion List)
Address: listserv@listserv.aol.com
Body: sub INBUSINESS <firstname lastname>

NDSRB-L (Students for Responsible Business)
Address: listserv@vma.cc.nd.edu
Body: sub NDSRB-L <firstname lastname>

NEWCOM-L (New Communication Technology)
Address: listserv@american.edu
Body: sub NEWCOM-L <firstname lastname>

ORGCOMM (Communication in Organizations)
Address: listserv@vm.its.rpi.edu
Body: sub ORGCOMM <firstname lastname>

PHILCOM (Philosophy of Communication)
Address: listserv@vm.its.rpi.edu
Body: sub PHILCOMM <firstname lastname>

VISCOM (Visual Communications Discussion)
Address: listserv@vm.temple.edu
Body: sub VISCOM <firstname lastname>

Business Usenet Newsgroups

> ## NOTE
> The ClariNet Hierarchy is a different type of
> newsgroup in that it is a read-only group. It is like
> a newswire service that has pre-selected articles
> relating to one subject area. Not all Internet sites
> have ClariNet since there is a charge at the
> institution level for receiving it.

Business And Business Communication

alt.business.import-export - Business aspects of international trade
alt.business.multi-level - Multi-level (network) marketing businesses
aus.comms - Discussion about communications in general
clari.biz.briefs - Business newsbriefs
clari.biz.earnings - Businesses' earnings, profits, losses
clari.biz.features - Business feature stories
clari.biz.front_page - Top five business stories each day
clari.biz.headlines - Two-line summaries of top business stories
clari.biz.misc - Other business news
clari.biz.top - High-priority business news
clari.usa.gov.policy.biz - U.S. business and economic policy
fj.soc.media - Discussions on the social aspects of media for
              communication
misc.business.consulting - The business of consulting
misc.entrepreneurs - Discussions on operating a business.
misc.entrepreneurs.moderated - Entrepreneur/business topics
pnet.comp.datacom - Data communications for business
pnet.talk.ptech - Chaos and complexity as it relates to business
rec.outdoors.marketplace - All business related to the outdoors
soc.college.org.aiesec - The Int'l. Assoc. of Business and Commerce Students
uiuc.class.badmin490 - Seminar in Business Administration
uiuc.class.btw250hc - Principles of Business Writing
uiuc.class.btw250s3 - Principles of Business Writing

CHAPTER 7
Using Cyberspace for
Career Planning

Today more and more career development centers are using the Internet as a resource for career planning. Major career planning activities include self-assessment and career exploration. In this chapter, you will

➼ take a self-awareness journey to learn more about yourself and your personal and professional needs;

➼ research jobs that fit you as a person; and

➼ learn how to use the Internet for career exploration: communication with people, electronic publications, career resources, and professional services.

Self-awareness Journey

Self-assessment is the first step in career planning. Self-assessment is an important process that requires inner reflection. The goal of this reflective process is to help you develop a better understanding of your interests, talents, values, goals, aptitudes, abilities, personal traits, and desired lifestyle. You will use this information to help find a job that fits you as a person. This personal survey is very important in helping you become aware of the interrelationship between your personal needs and your occupational choices.

Start by identifying:

- your interests and what is important to you;
- what you enjoy doing in your free time;
- skills you learned in the classroom or from an internship that are related to your career interests;

- your accomplishments;
- abilities and capabilities;
- work experience related to your career interests;
- personal traits and characteristics;
- your strengths and weaknesses; and
- physical and psychological needs.

Ask these questions regarding career considerations:

- Where would you like to live? In a city, the suburbs, the country, the seashore, or the mountains?

- Is there a specific geographic location where you would like to live?

- How do you feel about commuting to work? Would you drive a long distance to work for the advantage of living outside of a city?

- Is the community that you live in important? For example, do you value a community that is outdoor oriented or family oriented?

- What type of work environment is important to you? Do you want to wear a power suit every day or be casual?

- Is making a lot of money important to you?

- How do you feel about benefits and promotion options?

- Are flexible hours and free weekends important? For example, do you value free time to exercise and participate in outdoor activities? Are you willing to sacrifice this part of your life for a job? Would you be satisfied with making enough money to live on and have more free time?

- Do you mind working long hours each day or weekends? How do you feel about taking vacation time?

- Do you want to work for a large or small company? Would you rather work for a small company where everyone knows each other and the atmosphere is perhaps a little more casual? Or is it more important to be with a large company with many career advancement opportunities?

- Where would you like to be in your professional life in 5 years? 10 years? Does this company offer advancement opportunities that fit your goals?

- How do you feel about work-related travel? Do you mind traveling if a job requires you to do so? Do you mind giving up portions of your weekend to travel? How many days a month are you willing to be away from home?

- How do you feel about being a member of a work team?

After you have completed your self-awareness journey, you are ready to use this information to explore career options.

Career Exploration

The goal of career exploration is to help you to find job opportunities that match your personal and professional needs. Career exploration involves gathering information about the world of work. You will eliminate or select jobs based on what you learned in your self-assessment. For example, if you determine that location is an important factor when selecting a job, you would use this criteria to select or eliminate job opportunities based on where a particular company is located. Information about the work environment and corporate culture will be more difficult to obtain.

There are many ways to obtain information about the world of work. In this section we will explore several options involving communication and the use of the Internet to acquire information.

People as Information Resources

Internships and work experience provide excellent opportunities to learn about companies and their world of work. For example, if you are doing an internship for a company, observe the work ethic and corporate environment. Ask someone doing a job that interests you what it is like to work for the company. How many hours do they work per day? Are they expected to work weekends? How does their department, boss, and other employees view vacations? Do they have free time during a day for personal interests such as running, cycling, or working out at the gym? What are the company's expectations of its employees? If a job position requires the employee to travel, ask how many days per month they travel? When do they leave to travel; when do they return? How are they compensated for overtime?

Other sources for obtaining information from people include

- talking with your career counselors;
- attending seminars and workshops where you can interact with professionals and ask questions;
- attending conventions and job fairs;
- joining a professional organization; and
- NETWORK, NETWORK, NETWORK!

Publications as Information Resources

Professional publications provide valuable information about the world of work. Check with your career counselor or professors for publications that will provide useful information. Visit **Madlyn**—the Web site from the University of Deleware MBA Program—to find many links to current business news. **http://www.udel.edu/alex/mba/main/netdir2.html**

The **Electronic Newsstand** is another excellent resource with many links to electronic versions of publications. **http://www.enews.com**

The Internet as an Information Resource

The Internet has many valuable resources for learning about the world of work. Resources include:

- World Wide Web sites of companies
- Usenet newsgroups
- listserv mailing lists
- job and career resources

World Wide Web

Many companies have World Wide Web sites. You will find many of these Web sites useful in learning about a company's products and services and, in some instances, about their work environment. Use search engines described in Chapter 5 to help you find the home page of companies you are interested in. Listed below are Web sites to visit that have links to companies on the Internet.

Commercial Sites Index (**http://www.directory.net**) lists businesses that have set up home pages on the Web.

Interesting Business Sites on the Web (**http://www.owi.com/ netvalue/index.html**) is a relatively small list of sites (less than 50) that covers most of the exciting business uses of the Web.

The LIST (**http://www.sirius.com/~bam/jul.html**) is an excellent Web site with links to online businesses.

Usenet Newsgroups

In the virtual community of the Internet, Usenet newsgroups are analogous to a cybercafé where people with similar interests gather from around the world to interact and exchange ideas. Usenet is a very large distributed bulletin board system (BBS) that has several thousand specialized discussion groups. Currently there are over 20,000 newsgroups with about 20 to 30 more added weekly. Anyone can start a newsgroup.

> **NOTE**
> Your college or university must carry Usenet News
> before you can use your Internet browser to read
> and interact with newsgroups.

Listed below are several Usenet newsgroups that are relevant to job searching and career planning:

misc.jobs.contract
misc.jobs.misc
misc.jobs.offered
misc.jobs.offered.entry
misc.jobs.resumes

Netscape Navigator and Internet Explorer support Usenet newsgroups. To view all the newsgroups available on your college or university network, follow these steps from within Netscape Navigator 2.0 (for Explorer, see the online Help).

1. Click on the **Window** pull-down menu.
2. Select **Netscape News**.
3. Within the Netscape News window, go to the **Options** pull-down menu.
4. Select **Show All Newsgroups**.

Visit this Web site for a listing of Usenet newsgroups:
http://ibd.ar.com/ger

Visit this Web site and use a simple search tool to locate Usnet newsgroups of interest: **http://www.cen.uiuc.edu/cgi-bin/find-news**

For more information on using Netscape for reading newsgroups, refer to *Netscape Adventures—Step-by-Step Guide to Netscape Navigator and the World Wide Web.*

Listserv Mailing Lists

A *listserv* is the automated mailing system that distributes electronic mail. Mailing lists provide a forum where individuals of shared interests can exchange ideas and information; any members of the group may participate in the resulting discussion. This is no longer a one-to-one communication like your e-mail, but rather a one-to-many communication. Electronic mail written in the form of a report, article, abstract, reaction, or comment is received at a central site and is then distributed to the members of the list.

Finding a Listserv for Jobs and Career Planning

There are several Internet resources to help you to find a listserv mailing list for jobs or career planning.

http://www.yahoo.com/Business_and_Economy/Employment/Mailing_Lists

Two World Wide Web sites for finding mailing lists are:
http://www.liszt.com
http://www.tile.net/tile/listserv/index.html

Travel to this excellent Gopher server and follow the path to information on current mailing lists. You can also do a search for mailing lists by subject.

> Gopher: **liberty.uc.wlu.edu**
> path: Explore Internet Resources/Searching for Listservs

You can also use electronic mail to request information on listserv mailing lists on a particular topic. Send an e-mail message to:

LISTSERV@vm1.nodak.edu

In the message body, type: **LIST GLOBAL/*keyword***

For example, if you were looking for a mailing list on jobs you would type in the message body: **LIST GLOBAL/jobs**

TIPS for New Users of Newsgroups and Listservs

Tip 1...

After you subscribe to a list or newsgroup, don't send anything to it until you have been reading the messages for at least one week. This will give you an opportunity to observe the tone of the list and the type of messages that people are sending. Newcomers to lists often ask questions that were discussed at length several days or weeks before.

Tip 2...

Remember that everything you send to the list or newsgroup goes to every subscriber on the list. Many of these discussion groups have thousands of members. Before you reply or post a message, read and review what you have written. Is your message readable and free from errors and typos? When necessary, AMEND BEFORE YOU SEND.

Tip 3...

Look for a posting by someone who seems knowledgeable about a topic. If you want to ask a question, look for their e-mail address in the signature information at the top of the news article. Send your question to them directly rather than to the entire newsgroup or listserv.

Tip 4...

Proper etiquette for a mailing list is to not clog other people's mail boxes with information not relevant to them. If you want to respond to mail on the list or newsgroup, determine whether you want your response to go only to the individual who posted the mail or you want your response to go to all the list's subscribers. The person's name and e-mail address will be listed in their posting signature.

Tip 5...

The general rule for posting a message to a list or newsgroup is to keep it short and to the point. Most subscribers do not appreciate multiple-page postings.

If you are contacting an individual by electronic mail, identify yourself, state why you are contacting them, and indicate where you found their posting. Again, be as succinct and to the point as possible.

Request further information by either e-mail or by phone.

Job and Career Resources on the Internet

There are many excellent career planning and job-related resources on the Internet. Listed below are a few Web sites to investigate.

- **CareerMosaic**—Follow the links to the Resource Center
  http://www.careermosaic.com

- **Career Magazine**
  http://www.careermag.com/careermag

- **Monster Board Resource Link**
  http://199.94.216.76:80/jobseek/center/cclinks.htm

- **Occupational Outlook Handbook**
  http://www.jobweb.org/occhandb.htm

- **Online Career Center**
  http://www.occ.com

- **Riley Guide**
  http://www.jobtrak.com/jobguide/what-now.html

- **Survival Guide For College Graduates**
  http://lattanze.loyola.edu/MonGen/home.html

- **Tripod**—Tools for life to help you prepare for the real world
  http://www.tripod.com/tripod/

- **US Industrial Outlook**—Information on job market realities
  http://www.jobweb.org/indoutlk.htm

Professional Services as Information Resources

One valuable service to job seekers who want to learn what it's really like to work at a specific company or within a specific industry is Wet Feet Press. This service provides comprehensive in-depth analyses of companies at a cost of $25 per report. If you are currently enrolled as a Bachelor's or Master's student at a Wet Feet Press "Information Partnership" university, your cost is only $15 per report. As an alumnus of these universities, the cost is $20 per report. For more information call 1-800-926-4JOB. Visit the career center at your university or college to see if it belongs to Information Partners. For information on becoming an Information Partners member, call 415-826-1750.

The National Business Employment Weekly

The National Business Employment Weekly, published by Dow Jones & Company, Inc., is the nation's preeminent career guidance and job-search publication. It offers all regional recruitment advertising from its parent publication, *The Wall Street Journal*, as well as timely editorials on how to find a new job, manage the one you have, or start a business. You will find information on a wide range of careers. You will also get the latest on business and franchising opportunities, and special reports on workplace diversity. To view additional NBEW articles, subscription information, and job hunters' résumés, go to **http://www.occ.com/occ**

CHAPTER 8
Using Cyberspace to Find a Job

In this chapter, you will learn how to

- ↠ find companies with job opportunities;
- ↠ use the Internet as a tool for learning about job resources;
- ↠ develop résumés to showcase talent and skill;
- ↠ find Internet sites to post your résumé with;
- ↠ use the Internet as a tool to maximize your potential for finding a job; and
- ↠ prepare for a job interview by researching prospective companies.

The Internet provides new opportunities for job-seekers and companies to find good employment matches. Many companies are turning to the Internet believing that the people who keep up with the most current information and technological advances in their field are the best candidates for positions. The growing perception among employers is that they may be able to find better candidates if they search online.

The types of jobs offered on the Internet have changed dramatically over the last ten years. In the past, job announcements were primarily academic or in the field of science and technology. Now, thousands of positions in all fields from graphic artists to business and marketing professionals, from medical professionals to Internet surfers and Web programmers, are being advertised.

Many companies realize the impact of the digital revolution on business and are searching for professionals who are already online cybersurfing, networking with peers, researching information, asking questions, and learning collaboratively from others around the world. A number of companies report difficulty finding such qualified individuals.

How Can the Internet Help Me Find a Job?

The Internet provides an abundance of job resources including searchable databases, résumé postings and advertising, career planning information, and job-search strategies. There are several databases and newsgroups that allow you to post your résumé at no cost. Many companies post job listings on their Web pages.

The Internet also encourages networking with people around the country and around the world. People that you meet on the Internet can be important resources for helping you to find a job and learn more about the business or career you are interested in.

Each day, the number of job openings increases as new services become available. Many believe that the real changes and opportunities are still to come. The question is no longer whether the Internet should be used to find a job or an employee, but rather, how to use it.

How Do I Begin?

Listed below are a few ways to use the Internet in your job search:

- Visit Web sites with business resources or links to online companies. For example, Intel (**http://www.intel.com**) has information on job opportunities within the company (**http://www.intel.com/intel/oppty/us.htm**) as well as information on how to submit a résumé.

- Research companies that you are interested in by finding and exploring their Web pages.

- Learn more about job resources, electronic résumés, and employment opportunities available on the Internet.

- Create an electronic résumé.

- Use the Internet to give yourself and your résumé maximum visibility.

- Participate in Usenet newsgroups and listserv mailing lists to network and learn about companies you are interested in working for.

- Learn as much as possible about a prospective company before going for a job interview.

Seven Steps to Internet Job Searching

STEP 1

Research companies or organizations that you are interested in by finding and exploring their Web pages. There are many ways to find companies to match your personal and professional needs. Use the information from your self-assessment to refine and define your search for companies. Use both online and off-line resources. Listed below are sources to assist you with finding companies.

- Go to your library and review publications in your field of study. Look for classified ads in these publications. Find names of companies that interest you. Research these companies using the search tools you learned in Chapter 5.

- Search the classified section in newspapers in the cities or regions where you would like to live. Use the Internet to research these companies.

- Use Internet search tools described in Chapter 5 to find companies and employment opportunities. Begin by using broad terms such as *employment* or *employment and business*. If you are looking for employement opportunities in business communication, you might enter in a keyword that describes a job position, such as—*accountant, management training, office manager, sales*—or if you know the name of the company, do a search entering the company name as your keyword.

107

Visit these Web sites to find links to Internet resources for helping you to find business employemnt opportunities.

Infoseek Guide
http://guide.infoseek.com
Use the search engine and enter the word "employment."

World Wide Web Virtual Library
http://www.w3.org/hypertext/DataSources/bySubject/Overview.html

Yahoo
http://www.yahoo.com/yahoo/Business/Employment/Jobs/

STEP 2

Explore job resources and employment opportunities available on the Internet. Many Web sites have job postings and information on how to write résumés and effectively use the Internet for finding a job. Listed below are several excellent Internet resources to help you begin.

Best Bets for Extending Your Search: Other Internet Job Guides
http://www.lib.umich.edu/chdocs/employment/
This guide pulls together the Net's best sources of job openings and career development information, along with a description and evaluation of each resource.

Employment Opportunities and Job Resources on the Internet
http://www.jobtrak.com/jobguide
Margaret F. Riley's Web site has excellent job resources. A MUST VISIT Internet stop.

JobHunt: A Meta-list of Online Job-Search Resources and Services
http://rescomp.stanford.edu/jobs.html

- **Job Search and Employment Opportunities: Best Bets from the Net**, Phil Ray and Brad Taylor, University of Michigan SILS
  http://asa.ugl.lib.umich.edu/chdocs/employment

- **Job Search Guide**
  gopher://una.hh.lib.umich.edu/00/inetdirsstacks/employment%3araytay

- **RPI Career Resources   http://www.rpi.edu/dept/cdc**

- **Survival Guide For College Graduates**
  http://lattanze.loyola.edu/MonGen/home.html
  This award winning Web site (Fig. 8.1) has valuable information for college graduates seeking employment.

- **YAHOO Employment Resources**
  http://www.yahoo.com/Business_and_Economy/Employment/

FIGURE 8.1
Web page for A Survival Guide for College Graduates

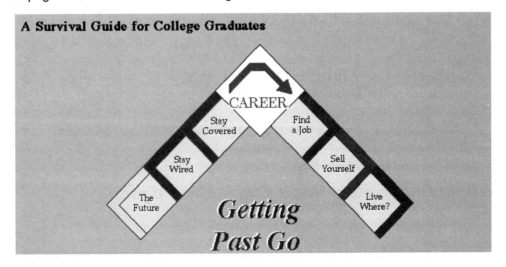

Usenet newsgroups and listserv mailing lists are two other Internet resources for learning about employment opportunities and for finding out how to find the information you are searching for.

STEP 3

Learn about electronic résumés. The World Wide Web has created opportunities for new types of résumés and business cards. Those who take advantage of the power of this new medium stand out as being technologically advanced and in touch with the future.

Listed below are Web sites to visit to examine online résumés. The individuals who have created these résumés understand how to use the medium to sell themselves. At the same time, they are stating that they have special skills for this new marketing medium that set them apart from other candidates.

Visit these Web sites and study these online résumés. Ask yourself the following questions as you look at them:

- How are online résumés different from traditional résumés?

- How do online résumés have an advantage over traditional résumés?

- What are some characteristics of the Internet as a medium that can be used to your advantage when designing a résumé to sell yourself to a company?

- How are these individuals taking advantage of the Internet as a medium to communicate?

- What do you view as advantages of using online résumés?

Sample Online Résumés and Home Pages

John Lockwood's Home Page
http://ipoint.vlsi.uiuc.edu/people/lockwood/lockwood.html

Mike Swartzbeck Home Page
http://myhouse.com/mikesite/

- Sandra L. Daine—Web designer, author, editor
  http://q.continuum.net/~shazara/resume.html

- Jon Keegan—Illustrator
  http://web.syr.edu/~jmkeegan/resume.html

- Allan Trautman—Puppeteer and actor
  http://www.smartlink.net/~trautman

- Ricardo Araiza—Student
  http://pwa.acusd.edu/~ricardo/resume.html

- Kenneth Morril—Web developer
  http://webdesk.com/resumes/kjmresume.html

- Laura Ann Wallace—Attorney
  http://lagnaf.isdn.mcs.net/~laura

Visit CareerMosaic to learn more about what online résumés look like and what they will look like in the future.
http://www.careermosaic.com/

Then go to the Career Resource Center. Send e-mail to these individuals and see if they have received job offers. Ask them about the responses they have received from their Web sites. How did they get maximum exposure to the Internet business community?

Visit Yahoo and explore links to résumé posting resources.
http://www.yahoo.com/Business_and_Economy/Employment/ Resumes

STEP 4
Visit online sites for job seekers. The next step is to visit Web sites that post résumés. Identify sites where you would like to post your résumé. There are many services available for job-seekers and for companies looking for employees. Companies usually pay to be listed; job-seekers may be allowed to post their résumés at no cost.

America's Job Bank
http://www.ajb.dni.us/index.html
This online employment service offers information on over 250,000 employment opportunities.

CareerMosaic
http://www.careermosaic.com
Begin your CareerMosaic tour by visiting the J.O.B.S. database, with thousands of up-to-date opportunities from hundreds of employers. Then stop by their USENET "jobs.offered" page to perform a full-text search of jobs listed in regional and occupational newsgroups in the U.S. and abroad. If you would also like to make your résumé accessible to interested employers from all corners of the globe, key into ResumeCM and post your résumé online.

Career Path
http://www.careerpath.com
Review employment opportunities from a number of the nation's leading daily newspapers such as *The New York Times*, *Los Angeles Times*, *The Boston Globe*, *Chicago Tribune*, *San Jose Mercury News*, and *The Washington Post*.

Career Resources Home Page
http://www.rpi.edu/dept/cdc/homepage.html
This Web site has links to online employment services including professional and university-based services.

CareerWeb
http://www.cweb.com
Search by job, location, employment, or keyword to find the perfect job. You can also browse employer profiles and search the Library's list of related publications.

E-Span
http://www.espan.com
E-Span, one of the country's foremost online recruitment services, provides tools designed to meet the needs of an increasingly competitive career market. Recently added to their services is Résumé

ProKeyword Database that is available to more than 60,000 individually registered career service consumers. Visit this Web site and select Job Tools.

Helpwanted.com
http://helpwanted.com
This site offers a searchable index of job openings for companies that have paid to be listed.

IntelliMatch
http://www.intellimatch.com
Connect to IntelliMatch and fill out a résumé; hundreds of employers will have access to your profile via the Holmes search software. Review other services such as job-related sites and products, participating companies, and descriptions of available jobs.

The Internet Online Career Center
http://www.occ.com
This career center and employment database is one of the highest-volume job centers with a long list of employment opportunities and resources. Post your résumé in HTML format. Use multimedia (images, photographs, audio, and video) to enrich your résumé.

JobHunt
http://rescomp.stanford.edu/jobs
An award-winning Web site with a Meta-list of On-Line Job-Search Resources and Services.

The Monster Board
http://www.monster.com/home.html
This unusual ad agency is a service for recruitment and furnishes information for job-seekers.

National Employment Job Bank
http://www.nlbbs.com/~najoban/
Executive Search of New England is pleased to post current career opportunities on its newest service, The National Employment Job Bank. These positions are current and represent some of the finest

employers and employment services in the country. There is never a fee charged to any applicant. These positions will be from nearly all states in the U.S.

Stanford University
http://rescomp.stanford.edu
Stanford University's site provides listings of online job services such as Medsearch and the Chronicle of Higher Education. They also have links to other agencies.

YahooJobs
http://www.yahoo.com/yahoo/Business/Employment/Jobs/
Many excellent links to help you find a job.

STEP 5
Create an online résumé to showcase your talents. In Steps 1-4, you learned about

- companies that fit your career interests;
- job and career resources on the Internet;
- electronic résumés and how they can showcase talents; and
- Web sites for job seekers.

You are now ready to use this information to create your own electronic résumé to showcase your talents and skills. Well designed and interesting online résumés set creative job seekers apart from others. When many individuals are competing for the same job, it is essential to stand apart and showcase your talents as to how they will benefit a company, especially in a time when businesses realize the importance of being networked to the world.

Creating an exceptional online résumé takes planning and careful thought. Online résumés take different form. Some may be an electronic version of a text-based résumé. Others may be home pages with links to resources that showcase a person's work and expertise.

114

Preparing Your Résumé for the Internet

Before you begin, think about your goals and what you would like to accomplish with an online résumé. Your primary goal is hopefully to find a job and not just to impress friends with a cool Home Page.

You will need to determine whether to create your online résumé yourself or hire a résumé service. If you are creating an electronic résumé on your own, consider whether you want to develop your own Home Page for your résumé or use an online database service to post your résumé. If you plan to create a Home Page you will need to learn HTML programming or use a software application program that creates an HTML code from your text. There are many software programs to assist you with this, as well as word processing programs that convert text to HTML.

If you are using an online résumé service, find out what type of text file they want. Usually, you will be asked for ASCII text. Most word processors and résumé writing programs have options for saving a file as ASCII or plaintext.

Investigate Résumé Services

Consider using a résumé service to create an online résumé. One advantage of using a service is that you may be able to get your résumé online quickly with instant exposure to many job opportunities. One disadvantage of using a service is that you do not have as much control over how your résumé will look. You may not be able to use complex graphics or other multimedia effects when using a service.

Cost is another limiting factor. Some companies charge a monthly fee to post your résumé, in addition to a set-up and sign-on fee. Look for companies that charge a reasonable fee to write a résumé ($35 - $50) and no fee to post it on their Web site. Investigate what other services they provide. How many visitors does this site have each day, each week? Will this site give you maximum exposure to potential employers?

Visit Web sites with résumé services. Evaluate their services: How many online résumés are posted? Are the résumés well done, creative, interesting? How well do they promote the job seeker?

115

Whether you choose to use a résumé service or to create your own online résumé, there are seven essential elements to follow.

The Seven Essential Elements of Electronic Résumés

1. Text must be properly formatted as an ASCII text file.

Using ASCII ensures that your résumé can be read universally by everyone and that readers will be able to scroll through your text. Additionally, an ASCII document can be e-mailed to anyone in the world and read.

2. Showcase your experience and education.

At the top of your résumé, provide links to your experience and education. Experience is usually the first thing employers look for. A fancy résumé will not help you get a job if you do not have the right qualifications. Notice that many online résumés provide examples of their work.

3. Provide an e-mail hyperlink.

An e-mail hyperlink provides an easy way for prospective employers to contact you by e-mail. By clicking on the link, they can send you a message, ask questions, or request additional information. Anything that makes it easier for recruiters improves your chances of being called for an interview.

4. Use nouns as keywords to describe your experience.

When employers use the Internet to search for qualified individuals, they will frequently use search engines that require keywords. The keywords used by employers are descriptors of the essential characteristics required to do a job, such as education, experience, skills, knowledge, and abilities. The more keywords that your résumé contains, the better your chances of being found in an electronic database.

116

Action words such as *created, arbitrated, managed, designed*, and *administered* are out. Therefore, use words such as *manager, law enforcement, accountant, MBA*. The use of nouns will tend to produce better results.

5. **Use white space.**
   An electronic résumé does not need to be one page long and single spaced. The use of white space makes reading easier and is visually more appealing. Use space to indicate that one topic has ended and another has begun.

   If you are a new graduate, a résumé equivalent of one page is appropriate. For most individuals with experience, the equivalent of two pages is the norm. Individuals who have worked in a field for many years may use two to three pages.

6. **Keep track of the number of visitors to your page.**
   A counter will keep track of the number of visitors that view your page. A counter is important when paying for a résumé service, to monitor how successful the service is with getting exposure for your résumé.

7. **Be sure your page gets maximum exposure to potential employers.**
   One way that employers look for prospective employees is to do a keyword search using search engines such as Yahoo, Excite, and Alta Vista. Each search engine uses a different criteria for selection of Internet resources that are available in their database. Be sure that your page is listed with search engines. Visit search engine Web sites and learn how to submit your page. Additionally, investigate the selection criteria for these search engines.

■ ■

Other Points to Consider

- Think of creative ways to show your talents, abilities, and skills. World Wide Web pages are excellent for linking to examples of your work.

- REMEMBER that experience is perhaps the critical element for recruiters. Be sure your résumé showcases your experience and skills in as many ways as possible.

- Visit the top 10-15 companies that you are interested in working for. Research their World Wide Web Home Page. Learn as much as possible about the company. Use this information when designing and creating your résumé to include information and skills that the company is looking for in its employees. Use this information before you go for an interview to show your knowledge and interest in the company.

- Investigate whether you will be able to submit your résumé electronically to the company.

- Are you concerned about confidentiality? Inquire about who will have access to the database you are posting your résumé with. Will you be notified if your résumé is forwarded to an employer? If the answers to these questions are not satisfactory to you, reconsider posting with this database.

- Once you post your résumé, anyone can look at it and find your address and phone number. You may want to omit your home address and just list your phone number and an e-mail hyperlink. Many recruiters and employers prefer to contact individuals by phone; if you decide not to post your phone number, you may be overlooked.

- Can your résumé be updated at no cost? You may want to add something to your résumé or correct a typo. Look for services that do not charge for updates.

- How long will your résumé be posted with the service? A good service will delete résumés after 3 to 6 months if they have not been updated.

STEP 6

Use the Internet to give yourself and your résumé maximum visibility. Successful job searches using the Internet require an aggressive approach. A résumé should be filed with many job-listing databases as well as with companies that you are interested in working for. Listed below are additional guidelines for giving yourself maximum exposure using the Internet.

- File your résumé with as many databases as possible. Visit the Net Sites for Job Seekers and find as many sites as possible to submit your résumé to.

- Use search engines and their indexes to locate resources specific to your occupation of interest.

- Visit the Home Pages of companies that you are interested in and explore their pages to find job listings. Find out if you can submit your résumé to them electronically.

- Use Usenet newsgroups and listserv mailing lists for information on finding jobs and posting your résumé.

Listed below are several Usenet newsgroups to investigate for posting résumés.

biz.jobs.offered
misc.jobs.contract
misc.jobs.misc
misc.jobs.offered
misc.jobs.offered.entry
misc.jobs.resume

STEP 7

Learn as much as possible about a prospective company before going for a job interview. Before going for a job interview, it is important to learn as much as possible about the prospective company. The Internet

119

is an excellent tool to assist you with finding up-to-date information about a company. Annual reports and information found in journals, books, or in the library will not be as current as what you will find on the Internet. World Wide Web sites are constantly being changed and updated.

The information that you should be investigating about a prospective company includes:

- What are the company's products and services?
- Who are the company's customers?
- What is the size of the company? Has the company grown over the last five years?
- Is the company profitable?
- Has the company laid off employees?
- How do customers and competitors view the company's products and services?
- Who are the company's major competitors?
- What is the corporate culture like?
- Is the employee turnover rate low, high, or average?
- Are work schedules flexible?
- How many hours a day do employees work?
- What is the typical hiring process?
- Is the organization non-profit or for-profit? There are differences in how these types of organizations operate.

CHAPTER 9
Guided Tour...
Using the Internet for Career Exploration and Job Opportunities

This chapter provides a guided tour of

- how to use the Internet for career exploration;
- how to use the Internet to find job opportunities in business;
- World Wide Web sites to explore for employment and job opportunities;
- Internet resources for finding information on companies; and
- Internet Business Directories.

Job Search 1 uses Internet resources for finding a job in management training. You will also learn how to research companies with posted jobs to learn more about their corporate culture and work environment.

Job Search 2 uses different Internet resources for finding information on job opportunities for accounting.

Job Search 1

Finding Employment Opportunities—
Management Training

There are many excellent Internet resources for assisting you with your career exploration. This guided tour takes you on a journey to Web sites with career and business resources for employment opportunities in management training. The same resources can be used for finding other business jobs for which you are qualified.

> ## NOTE
> There are many ways to find employment opportunities and information about businesses. The more knowledgeable you are about using Internet resources for finding information, the more options you will have open to you. This example merely serves as one pathway you might take.

STEP 1

Explore job opportunities. Visit Internet's Online Career Center to search for management training jobs by keyword search.
http://www.occ.com/occ

FIGURE 9.1
Online Career Center's Home Page to find job opportunities

This resource has links to Frequently Asked Questions, Jobs, Résumés, Career Fairs and Events, Career Assistance, and much more. Before you begin, you may want to explore some of these links. Visit the Career Assistance Center for information on writing electronic résumés and how to submit a résumé to the Online Career Center.

STEP 2

Search for a job. Use the search tool at this site to search for management training employment opportunities. In the **Keyword Search** field, type in the job description; in this case, *management training*. Click on the **Search** button. See Figure 9.2 for the results of this search.

FIGURE 9.2

Search results from the Online Career Center using keywords, *management training*

```
14.  [Jun 24] US-PA-Network Administrator- AAA Mid-Atlantic
15.  [Jun 24] US-MARKETING and SALES PROFESSIONALS- RCI NATIONAL SEARCH
16.  [Jun 24] US-MARKETING and SALES PROFESSIONALS- RCI NATIONAL SEARCH
17.  [Jun 24] US- MARKETING and SALES PROFESSIONALS- RCI NATIONAL SEARCH
18.  [Jun 24] US-MARKETING and SALES PROFESSIONALS- RCI NATIONAL SEARCH
19.  [Jun 24] US-MARKETING and SALES PROFESSIONALS- RCI NATIONAL SEARCH
20.  [Jun 24] US-MARKETING and SALES PROFESSIONALS- RCI NATIONAL SEARCH
21.  [Jun 24] US-NY-Director of Corporate Sales - OMNIPOINT
22.  [Jun 24] US-NY-Customer Service Team Leader - OMNIPOINT
23.  [Jun 24] US-NY-Manager - Customer Service Training - OMNIPOINT
24.  [Jun 24] US-PA-Customer Support Specialists- Delta Health Systems
```

When you click on the link to <u>Manager—Customer Service Training OMNIPOINT</u> you are given this information about the job.

```
Later this year, OMNIPOINT will be the first provider of PCS
services in the greater New York area,
bringing on a new era of advanced DIGITAL WIRELESS
COMMUNICATIONS and innovative services.
We are seeking a few highly accomplished individuals, from
both inside and outside the wireless industry,
to fill out a senior management team that is already unrival
in the industry.

Develop and customize customer service, billing, P/C trainin
programs. Facilitate programs developed
internally and monitor their effectiveness through analysis.
```

STEP 3

Note companies of interest. List companies of interest from your search. You will use the Internet to research these companies to learn more about them. For example, in the search results for management training opportunities, the company OMNIPOINT may have interested you. Note their name to research them on the Internet.

STEP 4

Learn about companies where jobs are offered. There are many ways to learn more about companies. In this instance, we will use the search engine, Excite, to research Omnipoint to learn more about the company, its products, and services. The search produces a link to the Omnipoint Home Page.

FIGURE 9.3

Excite search for Omnipoint links to the company's Home Page

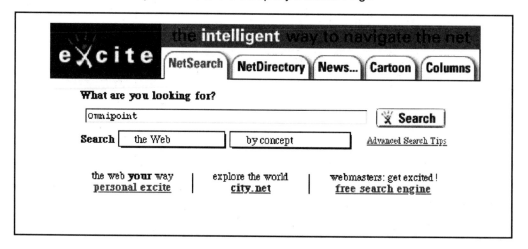

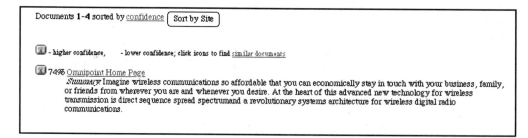

FIGURE 9.4
Omnipoint Home Page

Welcome To Our Home Page

LEARN MORE ABOUT OUR TECHNOLOGY

Imagine wireless communications so affordable that you can economically stay in touch with your business, family, or friends from wherever you are and whenever you desire. Affordable wireless communications without the interference or dropped calls often associated with conventional cellular technology. Imagine safe, secure communications and data transfer at speeds recently thought to be unobtainable.

At Omnipoint Corporation, our engineers have done more than merely imagine --- they've developed and produced systems that do all this, and more.

At the heart of this advanced new technology for wireless transmission is **direct sequence spread spectrum** and a revolutionary **systems architecture** for wireless digital radio communications. The leader in the commercial development and implementation of this technology: **Omnipoint**.

Already, the communications industry is embracing Omnipoint's revolutionary personal communications system (PCS), which has now been tested in over 30 cities accross the US. Industry leaders, including America's largest telephone and cable television companies have also joined Omnipoint in entering the 21st century of wireless communication.

Even the Federal Communications Commision has recognized the potential of Omnipoint systems, with a prestigious Pioneer's Preference award --- an award granting Omnipoint a PCS operating license for the New York Major Trading Area (MTA) and it's population base of almost 27,000,000.

The job search information indicated that Omnipoint was located in Mountain Lakes, New Jersey. You may want to research this city or town to learn more about it. In Job Search 2, you will learn how to find information on a city.

Job Search 2

Finding Employment Opportunities—Accounting

As you explore and use career and job-related Internet resources, you will find that there is no single Web site that provides all the information and tools that you will need to help you find a job.

You will find that many Web sites have a search tool to help you locate jobs and companies. Before you conduct a search, be sure you understand how the search engine can be used most effectively to find information.

Select links to **Options** or **Help** to learn more about the search tool. Other pages will provide you with information on how to conduct a search.

STEP 1

Explore jobs opportunities. Visit America's Job Bank to search for employment opportunities in accounting.
http://www.ajb.dni.us/index.html

FIGURE 9.5
Home Page for America's Job Bank

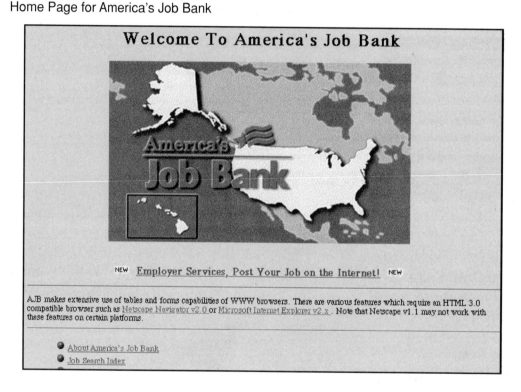

STEP 2

Select the link to the Job Search Index (shown in Fig 9.6). Select Keyword Search.

FIGURE 9.6

Clicking on the **Job Search Index** link takes you to the
Job Search Index Web page

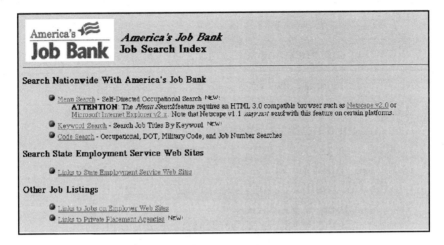

FIGURE 9.7

America's Job Bank page for finding a job by
location and job title

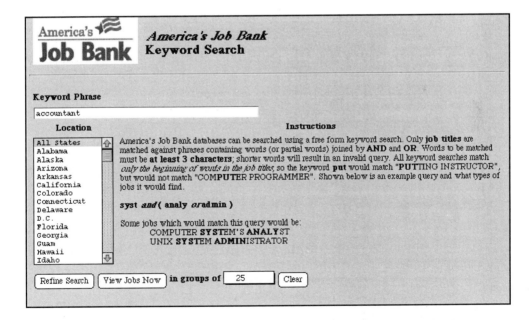

STEP 3
Select keyword search by job titles. Notice the difference in searching criteria used by the America's Job Bank in comparison to the Online Career Center.

Read the following instructions for conducting a search:

> America's Job Bank databases can be searched using a free form keyword search. Only job titles are matched against phrases containing words (or partial words) joined by AND and OR. Words to be matched must be at least 3 characters; shorter words will result in an invalid query. Listed below are examples of job titles.
>
> COMPUTER SYSTEMS ANALYST
> UNIX SYSTEM ADMINISTRATOR

FIGURE 9.8

Search results produced 286 leads for jobs
under the keyword *accountant*

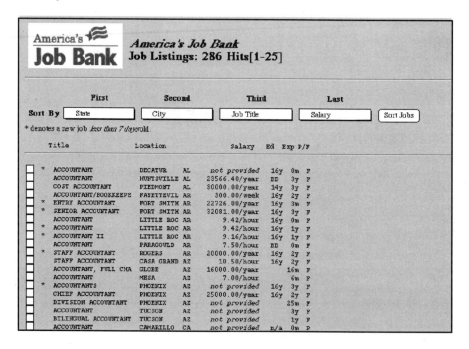

Notice that this search engine will sort jobs in an order that you select: city, state, job title, or salary. For this search, jobs were sorted first by state, then city.

To learn about each job, click once in the box next to each of the job postings you are interested in reading about. Then click on the button, **View Jobs**.

FIGURE 9.9
Job description for an accountant in San Francisco, California

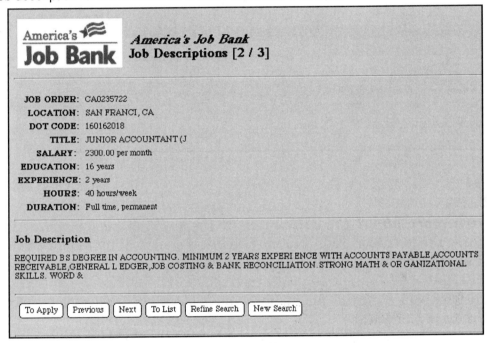

Click on the **Next** button for a job description of the second job you are interested in.

At the bottom of each page is a button to apply for the job if you feel you are interested and qualify. By selecting this option, you may learn more about the company or the recruiter posting the job.

FIGURE 9.10
Example of online application form for a job

America's Job Bank
America's Job Bank
Internet Referral

If you meet the employer's requirements and wish to apply for this job, please enter your name below. To apply you must be a U.S. Citizen or an individual authorized to work in the United States.

Job Number: CA0235722

Name:

Social Security #:

Once entered, you should print this panel and attach it to your resume/statement of qualifications and either fax or mail them both to the employment service order holding office at:

CALIF. EMPLOYMENT DEV. DEPT.
P.O. BOX 491329
REDDING, CA, 96049
FAX: (916)-225-2458

Please do not call this office. They will review your information and send it to the employer. If the employer is interested, you will be contacted directly.

[Enter Information] [Previous] [Next] [To List] [Refine Search] [New Search]

STEP 4
Learn more about the cities where these jobs are located. After reading the job description you may be interested in applying for the job, but would first like to learn more about the city where the job is located.

To learn about the cities for the jobs you selected, visit City Net.
http://www.city.net

This Web site (Fig. 9.11) provides options for learning about cities by visiting their Most Popular U.S. City Destinations or by conducting a keyword search.

Several of the accounting jobs were located in San Francisco, California. Select the link to San Francisco under Most Popular U.S. Cities (Fig. 9.12) or click on the search button and enter **San Francisco, California.**

FIGURE 9.11

Web site for City Net

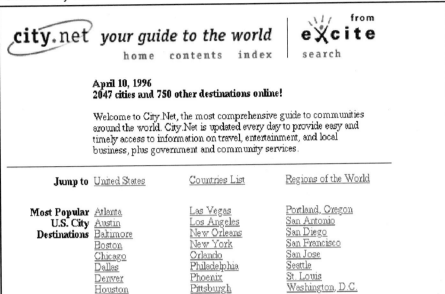

FIGURE 9.12

City Net's links to San Francisco information

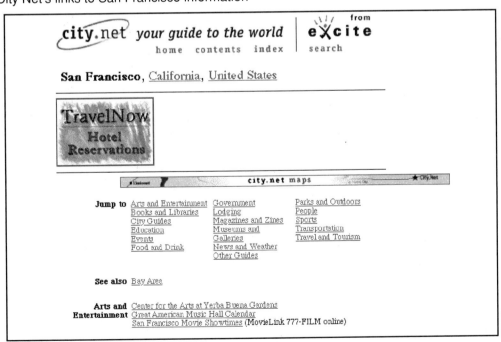

STEP 5

Use other career and job resources to search for jobs. Two other excellent Internet sites to assist with finding jobs are Career Web and Monster Board. Their job searches differ from Online Career Center and America's Job Bank. Enter in this URL for Career Web.
http://www.cweb.com

FIGURE 9.13
Career Web's search tool for finding a job by discipline and state/country

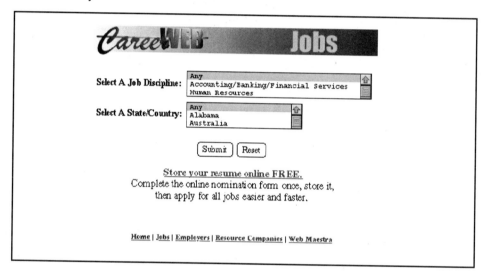

Notice that this job site asks you to select a job discipline and a state or country of your preference. Scroll down through the job disciplines to find one that best matches the job you are searching for. For your first search you may want to select Any State/Country to see what is available. Later you can refine your search.

STEP 6

Visit Monster Board to investigate its job search resources.
http://www.monster.com is its URL. When you connect to Monster Board, sign in as a first-time visitor. There is no charge for using and visiting this site.

After clicking on the two links, job opportunities and career search, you are at the page shown in Figure 9.14.

This job site presents job locations and job disciplines for you to select. For more information on each job discipline, click on the link for more information. After you select a location and discipline and conduct a search, you may be asked to refine your search. Monster Board also has options for keyword searches.

NOTE

After using four different Internet job resources, you now have some knowledge about Internet tools for finding job opportunities. You should also have a better understanding of how these resources differ in helping you to find a job. As with all Internet resources, you will need to use many different tools to help you find the information you are searching for. You will find that some tools are more helpful than others for specific types of information requested.

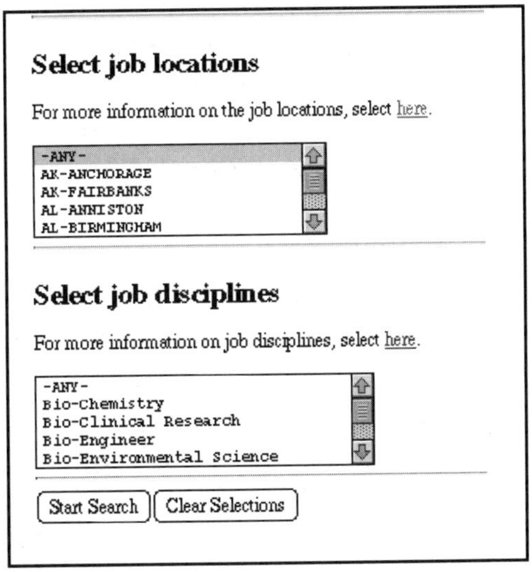

FIGURE 9.14

Monster Board's search options using location and job discipline criteria

Select job locations

For more information on the job locations, select here.

```
-ANY-
AK-ANCHORAGE
AK-FAIRBANKS
AL-ANNISTON
AL-BIRMINGHAM
```

Select job disciplines

For more information on job disciplines, select here.

```
-ANY-
Bio-Chemistry
Bio-Clinical Research
Bio-Engineer
Bio-Environmental Science
```

[Start Search] [Clear Selections]

Internet Resources To Explore

Employment and Job Opportunities

Refer to pages 112-114 for the best Internet resources to explore to help you find career and job opportunities.

Internet Business Directories

Internet Business Directories are resources to find information on a company.

Apollo

This Web site provides options for searching for a company by country and keyword. **http://apollo.co.uk**

Linkstar

Linkstar provides keyword search options, plus a listing of categories for finding information. **http://www.linkstar.com**

New Rider's WWW Yellow Pages

New Rider's World Wide Web Yellow Pages offers business search options by keyword or by category. A keyword search for jobs produces numerous job-related links. **http://www.mcp.com/newriders/wwwyp**

Nynex Interactive Yellow Pages

The largest of the business directories has options for searching for companies by business location, category, or business name. **http://www.niyp.com**

Virtual Yellow Pages

The Virtual Yellow Pages is a comprehensive and easy-to-use directory of Web sites and information. **http://www.vyp.com**

World Wide Yellow Pages

World Wide Yellow Pages has a link to assist you with finding information on businesses. **http://www.yellow.com**

CHAPTER 10
Learning Adventures—
Learning to Use the Internet

• •

This chapter provides the following learning activities for applying and using the information presented in *Internet Investigations in Business Communication.*

- ➡ using an Internet browser to visit Web sites
- ➡ using Bookmarks to save your favorite Internet sites
- ➡ subscribing to a listserv mailing list
- ➡ exploring Usenet newsgroups
- ➡ exploring electronic chats
- ➡ using search tools to find information
- ➡ exploring cool business sites to learn how the business community is using the Internet
- ➡ a self-awareness journey to learn about career goals and interests
- ➡ using the Internet as a tool for career exploration
- ➡ using the Internet to find job opportunities
- ➡ learning about electronic résumés
- ➡ designing an electronic résumé
- ➡ using the Internet to research companies you are interested in working for

• •

Chapter 1: What Is the Internet?
The metaphorical Internet—traveling down the information superhighway.

1. Write a metaphor for the Internet.

2. Today there are between 30-50 million Internet users. How do you see the Internet impacting your life? Your career?

3. Being on the Internet means having full access to all Internet services: electronic mail, Telnet, File Transfer Protocol (FTP), and the World Wide Web. Make a map that illustrates your understanding of what it means to be connected to the Internet.

Chapter 2: Guided Tour—Internet Browsers
I'm not lost . . . I'm just exploring!

Visit these Web sites using either Netscape Navigator or Microsofts Internet Explorer.

http://espnet.sportzone.com
http://mosaic.larc.nasa.gov/nasaonline/nasaonline.html
http://www.cybertown.com
http://www.kbt.com/gc
http://www.microsoft.com
http://www.paris.org
http://www.timeinc.com/pathfinder/Greet.html

1. Make bookmarks of Web pages you would like to save.

2. Organize your bookmarks by categories by creating file folders.

3. How do you think that the Internet will be used in the future? For business? For personal use? In the field of business communication?

4. Design a personal Home Page that provides information about yourself.

5. How is the Internet being used for communication?

6. Is the Internet a useful tool or just a fun, new technology that produces the "Oh Wow . . . this is cool" experience?

7. Do you believe that the Internet has a role in the future for your career and professional life? If so, what?

8. What do you believe is the best application for the Internet?

9. Export your bookmarks to a floppy disk.

10. Import your bookmarks from a floppy disk to the computer you are using.

Chapter 4: Chatting on the Net
The Internet opens new doors to virtual communities where we step through the looking glass.

1. Visit this Web site and search for a listserv in your field of study.
   http://www.tile.net/tile/listserv/index.html

2. Subscribe to several listserv mailing lists.

3. Use Netscape to explore Usenet newsgroups. Look for 5-10 groups related to your field of study.

   Visit this Web site for a listing of Usenet newsgroups.
   http://ibd.ar.com/ger

   Visit this Web site and use a simple search tool to locate Usnet newsgroups of interest.
   http://www.cen.uiuc.edu/cgi-bin/find-news

4. Visit these Web sites to experience Internet chat.
   WebChat Broadcast System **http://wbs.net**
   HotWired **http://www.hotwired.com**
   The Palace **http:www.thepalace.comg**
   Globe **http://globe1.csuglab.cornell.edu/global/homepage.html**

5. Do you see a use for online chats for business in the future?

137

Chapter 5: Finding Information and Resources
Traveling the Internet without getting caught in the Web

Select a topic of interest (i.e., a hobby, sport, country, a trip you plan to take, or a business communication issue).

1. Use Yahoo, Excite, Galaxy, and Magellan to research your topic. Begin by investigating their subject directories. After you have explored the directories, do a keyword search.

2. How do Yahoo, Excite, Galaxy, and Magellan differ in the way they provide access to information? Do you find one better or more useful than the other?

3. Explore the Advanced Options in Yahoo to refine and limit your search. Conduct a search using the Advanced Options. Did you get better returns?

4. Use each of the following search engines to research your topic: Excite, Alta Vista, Infoseek, and Open Text. Before you use these search engines, read how to use their advanced options for a more efficient search.

5. Compare and contrast Excite, Alta Vista, Infoseek, and Open Text. Which one did you find most useful in providing the information you were searching for? What are the advantages of each? Disadvantages?

6. How do search tools such as Yahoo and Magellan differ from search engines such as Excite, Alta Vista, Infoseek, and Open Text? Do you think there would be times you would find one more useful than another?

7. Begin a category or a file folder in your Internet browser for Internet research tools. Make bookmarks of search tools that you find helpful.

8. What does the future hold for Internet search tools?

138

Chapter 6: Cool Business Communication Web Sites

1. Journey into the cyberworld of business on the Net. Learn about how the information you are studying in your classes is applied and used in business communication. Explore the resources on page 73-89.

2. Identify an area of business communication you are interested in. Explore the electronics links to find more information in this area.

3. Research an electronic publication in business and keep up with its development and activities on the Internet.

4. How can the Internet add to your study of business communication?

5. Use the search tools you learned in Chapter 5 to research topics or issues you are studying in your classes.

6. How does the Internet as an interactive communication medium differ from traditonal media in providing business-customer communication services?

7. How do computers and networked computer systems change business-customer communication opportunities today?

8. Companies that view the Internet as just another communication medium lack an understanding of its strengths and capabilities. Discuss what this means to you.

9. Computers, computer-network systems, and the Internet are still being invented and defined for information access and global communication. Describe strategies for enhancing future customer communication using new digital interactive shared-space media.

Chapter 7: Using Cyberspace for Career Planning

The privilege of a lifetime is being who you are.
—Joseph Campbell

1. Write 25 things you love to do.

2. What do you do best?

3. What are your greatest achievements?

4. What do you find most rewarding when you work?

5. List and prioritize the 10 things that are most important to you. Which of these could you live without? Which of these are an essential part of your life that you cannot live without?

6. When you were a child, what did you want to be when you grew up?

7. What is your dream job now? Describe the perfect work environment. The perfect boss.

8. What is most important to you when evaluating a job?

9. List 5 jobs that incorporate the things you enjoy doing.

10. List 5 things that you would like to do at work.

11. List 5 ways that you will use people as a resource for learning about jobs and careers.

12. Subscribe to a Usenet newsgroup (page 100) and learn more about job opportunities.

13. After you have read the newsgroup postings, list 10 things you learned about job opportunities on the Internet.

14. Find a listserv mailing list related to jobs or your field of study (page 101).

15. If you have participated in a Usenet newsgroup or a listserv mailing list, describe your experiences. What have you learned? What are the advantages/disadvantages of a newsgroup? A listserv?

16. Visit job and career resources on the Internet (pages 121-123). Describe information that you found useful.

Chapter 8: Using Cyberspace to Find a Job

To be successful, you must love what you do.
—Dottie Walters

1. Research five companies you are interested in working for. Use the search tools described in Chapter 5. Visit and explore their Web pages. List the products and services of these companies. What have you learned about their work environment? Do they post job openings? How do you apply for a job?

2. Explore job resources and employment opportunities available on the Internet. List 5 jobs that you find from Internet resources that are of interest to you.

3. Research the city/state where these jobs are located.

4. Learn about electronic résumés by visiting the Web sites with online résumés (pages 110-111). How are online résumés different from traditional résumés?

5. What characteristics of the Internet as a medium for communication and information-sharing can be used to showcase your talents and skills with an online résumé?

6. What are the advantages/disadvantages of online résumés ?

7. Design an online résumé that showcases your talents and skills.

8. Visit online sites for job seekers (pages 112-114). Explore their online résumés. Identify the sites where you would like to post your résumé. What features do you like about each site? What do you have to do to post your résumé? Is there a cost? How long will it be posted? How will you learn if your résumé is seen by prospective employers?

9. List 5-10 jobs you found on the Internet that you are intersted in. Research the city and state where they are located. Does the information on the Internet help you determine which of these jobs you are most interested in?

10. You are preparing for an interview with a company that you are interested in working for. You know that it is important to have as much knowledge as possible about this company before the interview. How will you obtain this information? Select one company that you would like to interview with. Research information on this company using the Internet.

CHAPTER 11
Learning Adventures
in Business Communication

This chapter provides learning activities for applying and using the information presented in *Internet Investigations in Business Communication* to the study of business communications.

- ➧ mastering communication technology
- ➧ communicating in a world of diversity
- ➧ communicating using electronic forms
- ➧ designing electronic forms for improved communications and information access
- ➧ writing for effectiveness
- ➧ writing informative, routine, and goodwill messages
- ➧ writing disappointing or unfavorable messages
- ➧ writing a persuasive or sales message
- ➧ planning and researching business reports and proposals
- ➧ preparing for a presentation
- ➧ organizing and writing reports
- ➧ organizing and writing proposals
- ➧ delivering an effective oral presentation
- ➧ communicating about employment—from résumé to interview

Mastering Communication Technology

The Internet is a revolutionary new communication technology that is redefining human communication, consumer behavior, and information sharing. Small businesses to large corporations are exploring this new medium, trying to better understand how to tap its potential for future success. One way to begin to better understand the power of the Internet

143

as a new tool for business is to visit business World Wide Web sites and analyze how they are promoting their company, communicating with customers, building relationships, sharing information, and, perhaps most importantly, the design elements that attract customers and keep them returning?

1. Visit two of the following World Wide Web sites. Observe how they are communicating with their customers and Web visitors. How is the Internet being used as a new tool for business communication?

    AT&T **http://www.att.com/net**
    Fidelity Investment **http://www.fid-inv.com**
    Southwest Airlines **http://www.iflyswa.com**
    Time Warner's Pathfinder **http://pathfinder.com**

    Write a paper discussing the Internet as a new technology for business communication. Include in your discussion:

    *   How is this company using the Internet to communicate with customers? What service is this site providing to its customers?

    *   What is being communicated?

    *   How does this company use this new medium differently than traditional media to communicate?

    *   Does the company attempt to build a relationship with its customer? How?

    *   Do you think this medium is being used effectively to communicate?

    *   Why would a potential customer want to visit this site?

    *   Does this Web site capture your attention? Why?

    *   What makes the site informative, easy to navigate, and persuasive? Or, what keeps this site from having these important features?

- Why would a customer want to return to this site?

2. How can the Internet improve communication with customers?

3. Discuss how you have changed the way you communicate with others in the last 10 years. How do you prefer to communicate? How do you think a customer prefers to communicate?

4. Work in small groups and discusss how can the Internet open new markets for a business?

5. Visit **Interesting Business Sites on the Web** at the following URL: **http://www.owi.com/netvalue/v1i1l1.html** How do these online companies communicate a message? How do they engage their visitor?

6. Define Internet communication.

7. The tools used for communicating with customers have changed dramatically in this decade. Prior to the 1980s communication was in person, by U.S. mail, or by telephone. In the 1980s new tools for one-to-one communication were introduced: express mail, fax, cellular phones, and computers. In the 1990s interactive communication, such as computer networks, interactive television, videoconferencing, and the Internet, has opened new doors to improve business-customer relations. Compare how products and services were delivered to customers prior to the 1980s, in the 1980s, and the 1990s, and how they will be delivered the year 2000. Include the advantages and/or disadvantages of communication tools of each time period.

8. How do you communicate with companies you buy products from? Describe good business-customer communication experiences you have had. Describe your bad experiences. How does this affect your loyalty to the company? How does it affect your satisfaction of the product?

Communicating in a World Of Diversity

1. CASE STUDY: You have just been employed by a company that does business in Africa. During your first week of orientation you have

been instructed to research Africa to help you to understand the people, culture, language, communication styles, and business practices. You decide to use the Internet as your tool for conducting research, realizing that you will have immediate access to information.

To begin your research, visit the following World Wide Web site for Afro Americ@: **http://www.afroam.org**

The Afro Americ@ site is the home of the AFRO-American Newspapers that have for the past 103 years reported and chronicled the events and issues relating to the African-American community. This site makes available many aspects of the massive collection of African-American history. Additionally, direct e-mail communication is available with various AFRO columnists, editors, and other staff.

Use Internet search engines to further your knowledge.

Write a two-page description of your research findings. Include in your paper the following:
- Overview of important cultural information that may affect your work with the company.
- How will the African culture, ethnocentrism, and language differences affect your communication?
- Describe any differences in business practices.

2. CASE STUDY: You have just been hired to develop a diversity training program for a company. You have been asked to develop units on African Americans, Hispanics, Native Americans, Asian Americans. You decide that the first step in learning more about these cultures is to conduct research on each. Visit the following World Wide Web sites to begin your research.

    Afro Americ@　　　**http://www.afroam.org**

    Native Web　　　**http://web.maxwell.syr.edu/nativeweb**

The Native Web site weaves a web that connects all beings. It provides information on indigenous people, focusing on how much we all have in common amidst great diversity. Here you will find information on native literature and art, legal and economic issues, and new ventures in self-determination. An important and valuable site to learn about other cultures.

Hispanic/Spanish
http://web.maxwell.syr.edu/nativeweb/geography/latinam/mexico/mex_main.html
Learn about the Hispanic culture from this top Web site: languages of Mexico; Mexican poetry/songs/dances; stories by native Mexicans; origins of Mexico; and much more.

Use Internet search engines to further your knowledge.When you have finished conducting your research, write a paper that includes:

- Cultural information that might tend to influence communication with African Americans, Hispanics, and Native Americans,and Asian-Americans. This information might include differences in attitudes, behaviors, and communication styles.

- How communication styles differ with each of these cultures.

Based on your research of African Americans, Hispanics,Native Americans, and Asian Americans design and write a training activity whose objective is the appreciation of cultural differences as assets for making the company stronger, more creative, and more productive.

Communicating Using Electronic Forms

The Internet uses many different types of electronic forms for communication. Visit the following sites to learn more about how forms are used and designed on the Internet.

Web Shopping Malls

Visit the following cybermalls and learn how electronic forms are being used for business.

Apollo Advertising (**http://apollo.co.uk**) in England uses forms for finding products, opening new accounts, sending in ideas, providing feedback, and ordering products.

- **Branch Information Services (http://branch.com:1080)** is one of the oldest and largest shopping malls on the Internet.

- **Interactive Super Mall (http://supermall.com)** uses e-mail autoresponders to make information available to customers. Visit this Web site to learn how these cyberforms enhance customer service.

- **Internet Plaza (http://plaza.xor.com)** This site is one of the Internet's premier locations for online commerce. The Internet Plaza, brought together some exceptional Web sites for you to browse and enjoy. Investigate its streets or proceed to PlazaTown for an overview of everything it has to offer.

Investment and Financial Services—Electronic Forms

Investment services use electronic forms to provide services to customers. Visit these investment sites and discover how they use electronic forms.

- **Dun & Bradstreet**
  http://www.dbisna.com
  Visit this award-winning site to see how this company is communicating with customers.

- **Fidelity Investment**
  http://www.fid-inv.com
  Forms include investor profiles and retirement worksheets.

- **First Union**
  http://www.firstunion.com
  Learn about cyberbanking with one of the first banks to provide services to customers online.

▣ Wall Street Direct
http://www.cts.com/~wallst
The Wall Street Directory contains over 2500 pages of information for computerized traders and investors, with more than 2000 products and services from companies and institutions—located both on and off the Internet. Visit this site to learn how forms are being used.

▣ Wells Fargo
http://wellsfargo.com
Since 1852, the Wells Fargo stagecoach has been a symbol of reliable service across the American West. Over one hundred years ago, their stages traveled across thousands of miles of desert, prairie, and mountain roads to deliver mail and cash. During the Gold Rush, they provided regular communications (including the first electronic transaction by telegraph in 1864), delivered vital goods, converted unprocessed gold into U.S. gold coins, and supplied checks and bank drafts. Today, Wells Fargo continues to lead the way in communication and financial services to customers 24 hours a day.

Search Engines—Electronic Forms
Search engines use electronic forms for finding information and resources on the Internet.

a. **Yahoo**   **http://www.yahoo.com/search.html**
b. **Lycos**   **http:/lycos.cs.cmu.edu**
c. **EINet**   **http://galaxy.einet.net/search.html**
d. **WebCrawler** **http:/www.webcrawler.com**
e. **Excite**   **http://www.excite.com**

Submitting Web Pages to Search Engines—Electronic Forms
a. **WebCom**   **http://www.webcom.com/~webcom/html/ publicize.html**
b. **HUGE List**   **http://thehugelist.com/addurl.html**
c. **Internet Yellow Pages**
            http://www.webcom.com/~webcom/html/ publicize.html

149

Application Activities

1. Print a copy of four different electronic forms. Write a paper in which you discuss the following:
   - What service do these forms provide to customers?
   - Compare and contrast how these forms differ from print forms?
   - How do these forms help companies to communicate?
   - How do forms contribute to increased customer services?
   - What are the advantages/disadvantages of electronic forms?

2. Survey potential customers regarding the use of electronic forms for communication and information requests. How will the organization be affected by the use of electronic forms? How does this change and affect the nature of customer service?

Designing Electronic Forms for Improved Communication and Information Access

1. The future of the Internet includes the development of tools to assist people with finding information and resources. Now that you have explored how the Internet is using forms for communication and information access, design a new and improved form for Internet research or for obtaining information from a company.

2. Describe the steps that you would take for planning, researching, organizing, and designing the research/information-request form. Begin by brainstorming the types of information that would be useful on this form. Define your objectives for this form, the purpose, the intended audience, and types of information requested on the form.

3. Work in groups or individually. Select one type of form commonly used in a business. Discuss how an electronic version of this form would affect customer service. Advantages/disadvantages. Design an electronic version of this form and discuss how the company will manage the electronic correspondence generated from this new form.

4. Survey potential customers to see how electronic forms would affect their company and customer service.

Writing for Effectiveness

Use the following Internet sites to connect to online companies for the next activities.

 EINet Galaxy Business and Commerce
http://www.einet.net/galaxy/Business-and-Commerce.html

 Global Network Navigator—Business Links
http://gnn.com/wic/wics/bus.new.html

 Interesting Business Sites
http://www.owi.com/netvalue

 World Wide Web Business Yellow Pages
http://www.cba.uh.edu/ylowpges/ycategor.html

 Yahoo—Business and Economy
http://www.yahoo.com/Business_and_Economy

1. Visit Internet business sites to analyze and evaluate the organization and presentation of information on their World Wide Web pages. Write a paper that includes the following:

   • Is information organized differently on the Internet than what you would expect in a company brochure? Describe.
   • How does the use of multimedia (images, video, sound) contribute to the clarity of the information?
   • How do the visual elements contribute to encouraging the visitor to read the Web document?
   • Do the documents use the five design elements?
   • How does document design differ on the Web from traditional print? How is it the same?

2. Work in small groups. On your own, visit business sites on the Internet. Explore these sites for opportunities to request information. Use the electronic mail option to send an electronic request for information from 2-4 companies.

   When you have received information from the companies, meet in your group and discuss the following:
   - How does the electronic request for information change the way services are provided to customers on the Internet?
   - What are the advantages of using the Internet for customer requests for information?
   - Is the nature and format of the information returned different from what you might expect by surface mail?

3. Send a written request by surface mail to the same company that you sent the electronic request to. Compare and contrast the type of information you received from both requests.

   The following Web sites have links to businesses on the Internet:

   - **EINet Galaxy Business and Commerce**
     http://www.einet.net/galaxy/Business-and-Commerce.html

   - **Global Network Navigator—Business Links**
     http://gnn.com/wic/wics/bus.new.html

   - **Interesting Business Sites**
     http://www.owi.com/netvalue

   - **The LIST**
     http://www.sirius.com/~bam/jul.html

   - **World Wide Web Business Yellow Pages**
     http://www.cba.uh.edu/ylowpges/ycategor.html

   - **World Wide Web Virtual Library for Finance and Investment**
     http://www.cob.ohio-state.edu/dept/fin/overview.htm

- **Yahoo—Business and Economy**
  http://www.yahoo.com/Business_and_Economy

Writing Informative, Routine, and Goodwill Messages

1. Work in small groups. Discuss whether e-mail is appropriate for each of the following goodnews and goodwill information messages: order acknowledgments, letters of credit, adjustment letters, positive personal letters, thank-you messages, congratulatory letters, condolence letters, greetings, and informative letters. What are the advantages/disadvantages of using electronic media for goodnews and goodwill messages?

2. Divide your group in half. Select one type of goodnews or goodwill information message. Group 1 will write the message to be delivered by e-mail; Group 2 writes the message to be delivered by surface mail. Compare and contrast the differences in both types of messages.

3. Many goodnews and informative letters are responses to inquiries. Goodwill can be communicated by the speed in which a company responds to an inquiry request. Visit Internet business sites and evaluate how this new media is changing or has the potential to change the quality of goodwill and customer service for information requests.

Writing Disappointing or Unfavorable Messages

1. Work in small groups. As more individuals and companies become connected to the Internet, e-mail is rapidly becoming the preferred way to communicate. Begin by discussing the ramifications of using e-mail vs. surface mail for the delivery of bad news and negative messages involving orders, credit, claim, request, invitations, and personnel issues. Will the message(s) be perceived differently when delivered by e-mail vs. surface mail? When would e-mail be appropriate? Inappropriate? Would your choice for the use of e-mail to communicate bad news be different when writing to a manager, co-worker, or subordinate?

2. Read and discuss the following e-mail message. Why do you think that it is easy for e-mail to have a negative or angry tone? How could this situation be handled differently? Is e-mail the best way to communicate in a situation such as this? Re-write this e-mail message.

> *I thought I left you a detailed voice mail message regarding the diversity training program. I was surprised that you did not respond due to the urgency of the situation. First of all only 4 managers showed up for the meeting, not 9 as you stated in your report. Yes I too was upset by the lack of interest shown by the managers but they should be motivated to attend these types of meetings. Please return my call and report to me your thoughts and opinions on why so few showed up.*

3. Companies that are internally networked frequently use e-mail to deliver messages to employees. Ask several individuals in your group to write a bad news message to be delivered by e-mail for one of the following situations:

   - Employees will not receive a raise this year.
   - A job applicant is not qualified for a management position
   - an employee is denied promotion.
   - A company no longer can provide financial support for a holiday party.
   - An employee's vacation request is denied.
   - A warrantee replacement part for a computer is backordered for one month.
   - An employee's e-mail message to his development team was inappropriate.

   Have the group respond to the message. How would they feel? Could the message have been better written for e-mail delivery? Would the tone of the message be different for a business letter?

4. Work in small groups for this case study. A small start-up Internet access provider is designing a Web page that will provide information for its customers. Designers are considering an interactive electronic

forum where their customers can give them feedback on their services. How might the company design this interactive service? How would they plan to followup with complaints, negative messages, and feedback?

Writing a Persuasive or Sales Message

1. You have been hired to work on the Internet team for a publishing company. Your assignment is to write a persuasive message that will be used in their print advertising to encourage people to visit the company's World Wide Web page. Write another persuasive message that can be used to announce the Web site to Usenet newsgroups. How will the message change for the different types of media?

Planning and Researching Business Reports and Proposals

1. The Internet has stimulated new discussions on copyright. Information is freely available to be downloaded, copied, and repurposed. Artists, musicians, writers, educators, businesses, and software developers are among the many who express concerns about having their work illegally copied. Discussions on Internet copyright are prolific. Some Internet users believe, "If you don't want your product copied, then don't put it on the Internet." Still others hold to "fair-use" standards—if the information is being used for educational purposes and not for your profit, this falls into the fair-use category and is acceptable.

   Use search engines described in Chapter 5 and research copyright issues on the Internet. Begin your research by visiting the Copyright Web site: **http://www.benedict.com**

   Make a list of the Web sites you visit. Include in this paper a list of Internet resources for your research: title of Web page and URL.

2. The Internet has many information services available online. Some require subscriptions for access to their databases. Hundreds of thousands of professionals worldwide perform searches using these services. Visit Internet sites where information is made available to

users from a database. How is this information made available? Is there a cost?

- **LEXIS-NEXIS**
  http://www-1.openmarket.com/lexis-nexis

- **Wall Street Directory**
  http://www.cts.com/~wallst
  http://www.wsrn.com
  http://wall-street-news.com/forecasts

- **PcQuote:**
  http://www.pcquote.com/aboutus.html

- **Library of Congress**
  http://lcweb.loc.gov/homepage/lchp.html

- **Dow Jones News**
  http://www.dowjones.com/djnr.html

- **Britannica Online**
  http://www.eb.com

After you have visited these sites, write a paper on "Online Information Services." Include information about the

- type of information service(s) provided;
- types of research services available;
- specialized libraries offered;
- cost;
- communication services for customers;
- advantages/disadvantages of using this service.

Preparing for a **Visual Presentation**

1. The Internet is being used more and more frequently for researching information for business reports and presentations. As you visit Web sites you will find images, charts, and graphs that will enhance your reports and presentations.

You will be assigned a topic by your professor to research a business report. Use the Internet search engines for this purpose. Find several images you would like to include in your business report. Before you can include these images, you must examine copyright issues. Expand your research on Internet copyright for information on permission to use the Internet visuals.

2. Visit Internet business sites and explore how visuals (graphics, maps, charts, graphs, and tables) are being used by companies to communicate a message. How are the visuals communicating a company message? What is the message? Are the visuals interactive? How do Web visitors interact with the visuals? How does this interaction affect communication or information access? Are all visual aids working effectively? Why? Write 5 guidelines for using visuals on a business Web page.

Organizing and Writing Reports

1. CASE STUDY: The company that you work for is interested in learning more about whether they should establish an Internet presence. They quote you the following statements:

    *   Business on the Net is not easy.
    *   Many dollars are wasted on Internet advertising.
    *   The Internet is a place you can't afford not to be right now. It's not so much that you're going to profit in the near term; rather, you'll lose money in the long term by not being there.
    *   If you're not an active Internet citizen by the mid-1990's, you're likely to be out of business by the year 2000.
    *   A Web site can provide you with a global presence with one click of the mouse.
    *   Putting up a Web site is like setting up shop in the middle of the desert.

    Your assignment is to research business practices on the Internet and write a short report for your boss with facts and recommendations regarding the advantages of your company establishing an Internet presence.

Organizing and Writing Proposals

1. CASE STUDY: After reading your report, management is very interested in setting up a World Wide Web site for the company. You have now been asked to write an internal proposal for the establishment and maintenance of a World Wide Web site. This proposal will include three new positions: Web programmer, graphic artist, and company content expert. Each of these positions does not need to be full-time. Include in your proposal the following:

   - Introduction (summarize your findings and recommendations from your previous research)
   - Technical plan
   - Management plan including cost analysis
   - Persuasive conclusion

Delivering an Effective Oral Presentation

1. You have been asked to prepare and deliver a presentation to the president, vice-president, managers, and sales staff of your company on your research findings and proposal for the company to establish a World Wide Web site. Prepare a 5-minute presentation. Include the visuals you will be using to emphasize the importance of establishing a Web presence. Be prepared to give the presentation to the class.

Communicating about Employment—from Résumé to Interview

1. The Internet is providing new opportunities for job-seekers and companies to find good employment matches. Many companies are turning to the Internet believing that the people who keep up with the most current information and technological advances in their field are the best candidates for positions. The growing perception among employers is that they may be able to find better candidates if they search online. Visit the Web sites listed in Chapter 8 and review online résumés. Print examples of different types of résumés that illustrate how the Internet is being used to showcase talents and skills. Be prepared to discuss online résumés in small groups.

2. In small groups discuss how the Internet changes the way résumés are designed, developed, and delivered. How does the Internet provide an advantage over others who are not using this medium for their résumé?

3. Design an online résumé for a job you are interested in. Post your résumé to online services.

4. Use one of the online job centers from Chapter 9 to find several jobs you would be interested in. Research the companies offering the jobs .

5. You are preparing for an interview with a company. Your preparation includes learning as much information as possible about the company. Research the company using search engines such as Excite or Alta Vista. Visit its Home Page and write a short description of the company that lists important information you should know for your interview.

GLOSSARY

applets: Mini-applications that a software program such as Netscape downloads and executes.

ASCII (text) files: One of the file transfer modes (binary is another mode) used when transferring files on the Internet. ASCII treats the file as a set of characters that can be read by the computer receiving the ASCII text. ASCII does not recognize text formatting such as boldface, underline, tab stops, or fonts.

binary file: Another transfer mode available for transferring Internet files. In the binary mode, files are transferred which are identical in appearance to the original document.

Binhex (BINary HEXadecimal): A method for converting non-text files (non-ASCII) into ASCII. Used in e-mail programs that can handle only ASCII.

Bit: A single-digit number, either a 1 or a zero, that represents the smallest unit of computerized data.

bookmarks: A feature providing the user with the opportunity to mark favorite pages for fast and easy access. Netscape's bookmarks can be organized hierarchically and customized by the user through the Bookmark List dialog box.

boolean operators: Phrases or words such as "and," "or," and "not" that limit a search using Internet search engines.

browser: A client program that interprets and displays HTML documents.

client: A software program assisting in contacting a server somewhere on the Net for information. Examples of client software programs are Gopher, Netscape, Veronica, and Archie. An Archie client runs on a system configured to contact a specific Archie database to query for information.

compression: A process by which a file or a folder is made smaller. The three primary purposes of compression are to save disk space, to save space when doing a backup, and to speed the transmission of a file when transferringover a modem or network.

domain name: The unique name that identifies an Internet site. Names have two or more parts separated by a dot such as **xplora.com**

finger: An Internet software tool for locating people on the Internet. The most common use is to see if an individual has an account at a particular Internet site.

fire wall: A combination of hardware and software that separates a local area network into two parts for security purposes.

frames: A new feature of Netscape Navigator 2.0 makes it possible to create multiple windows on a Netscape page. This is an example of a Web page divided into several windows called *frames*. To navigate within frames and to save bookmarks, you will use your mouse. To move forward and back within frames, position your cursor within the frame and hold down the mouse button (Macintosh users); Windows users hold down the right mouse button. A pop-up menu appears. 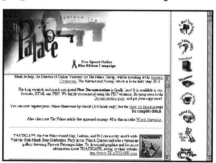 Choose **Back in Frame** or **Forward in Frame**. To bookmark a frame, place your cursor over the link to the frame and hold down the mouse button. A different pop-up menu appears. Select, **Add Bookmark for this Link**. To print a frame, click the desired frame and select **Print Frame** from the **File** menu.

FTP (file transfer protocol): Protocol for transferring files between computers on the Internet.

GIF (Graphic Interface Format): A format developed by CompuServe, Inc. for storing complex graphics. This format is one of two used for storing graphics in HTML documents.

Helper Applications: Programs used by Netscape to read files retrieved from the Internet. Different server protocols are used by Netscape to transfer files: HTTP, NNTP, SMTP, and FTP. Each protocol supports different file formats for text, images, video, and sound. When these files are received by Netscape, the external helper applications read, interpret, and display the file.

History List: Netscape keeps track of your Internet journeys. Sites that you visit are listed in the History List found under the **Go** pull-down menu. Click on an Internet site on your list, and you will be linked to that destination.

Home Page: The starting point for World Wide Web exploration. The Home Page contains highlighted words and icons that link to text, graphic, video, and sound files. Home Pages can be developed by anyone: Internet Providers, universities, businesses, and individuals. Netscape allows you to select which Home Page is displayed when you launch the program.

HTML (HyperText Markup Language): A programming language used to create a Web page. This includes the text of the document, its structure, and links to other documents. HTML also includes the programming for accessing and displaying media such as images, video, and sound.

HTTP (HyperText Transfer Protocol): One protocol used by the World Wide Web to transfer information. Web documents begin with **http://**

hyperlinks: Links to other Web information such as a link to another page, an image, or a video or sound file.

hypertext: A document containing links to another document. The linked document is displayed by clicking on a highlighted word or icon in the hypertext.

IP address: Every computer on the Internet has a unique IP address. This number consists of four parts separated by dots such as 198.68.32.1

JavaScript: A new programming language developed by Sun Microsystems that makes it possible to incorporate mini-applications called *applets* onto a Web page.

JPEG (Joint Photographic Experts Group): A file format for graphics (photographs, complex images, and video stills) that uses compression.

live objects: Java brings life and interaction to Web pages by making it possible to create live objects. Move your mouse over an image of a house and see the lights go on. Move your mouse to a picture of a woman and hear her welcome you to her Home Page.

MIME (Multimedia Internet Mail Extension): Most multimedia files on the Internet are MIME. The MIME type refers to the type of file: text, HTML, images, video, or sound. When a browser such as Netscape retrieves a file from a server, the server provides the MIME type to establish whether the file format can be read by the software's built-in capabilities or, if not, whether a suitable helper application is available to read the file.

newsgroups: Large distributed bulletin board systems that consist of several thousand specialized discussion groups. Messages are posted to a bulletin board by e-mail for others to read.

NNTP (News Server): A server protocol used by Netscape for transferring Usenet news. Before you can read Usenet news, you must enter the name of your news server to interact with Usenet newsgroups. The news server name is entered in the Mail and News dialog box (**Options** pull-down menu; **Preferences**; Mail and News).

page: A file or document in Netscape that contains hypertext links to multimedia resources.

platform: Netscape Navigator 2.0 is referred to as a platform rather than a browser. A platform program makes it possible for developers to build applications onto it.

PPP (Point-to-Point Protocol): A method by which a computer may use a high-speed modem and a standard telephone line to have full Internet access. A PPP or SLIP connection is required to use graphical interfaces with the Internet such as Netscape Navigator and Explorer. Using a PPP or SLIP connection enables you to point and click your way around the Internet.

.sea (self-extracting archives): A file name extension indicating a compression method used by Macintosh computers. Files whose names end in .sea are compressed archives that can be decompressed by double-clicking on the program icon.

search engine: Software programs designed for seeking information on the Internet. Some of these programs search by keyword within a document, title, index, or directory.

server: A computer running software that allows another computer (a client) to communicate with it for information exchange.

shell account: The most basic type of Internet connection. A shell account allows you to dial into the Internet at your provider's site. Your Internet software is run on the computer at that site. On a shell account your Internet interface is text-based. There are no pull-down menus, icons, or graphics. Some Internet providers offer a menu system of Internet options; others merely provide a Unix system prompt, usually a percent sign or a dollar sign. You must know the commands to enter at the prompt to access the Internet.

SLIP (Serial Line Internet Protocol): A method by which a computer with a high speed modem may connect directly to the Internet through a standard telephone line. A SLIP account is needed to use Netscape. SLIP is currently being replaced with PPP (Point-to-Point Protocol).

SMTP (Simple Mail Transport Protocol): A protocol used by the Internet for electronic mail. Before using Netscape e-mail, the host name of the Internet provider's mail server must be designated. The mail server name is entered in the Mail and News dialog box (**Options** pull-down menu; **Preferences**; Mail and News).

source file: When saved as "source," the document is preserved with its embedded HTML instructions that format the Internet page.

TCP/IP (Transmission Control Protocol/Internet Protocol): The protocol upon which the Internet is based and which supports transmission of data.

toolbar: Navigational buttons used in graphical interface applications.

URL (Uniform Resource Locator): URLs are a standard for locating Internet documents. They use an addressing system for other Internet protocols such as access to Gopher menus, FTP file retrieval, and Usenet newsgroups. The format for a URL is **protocol://server-name:/path**

URL object: Any resource accessible on the World Wide Web: text documents, sound files, movies, and images.

Usenet: Developed in the 1970s for communication among computers at various universities. In the early 1980s, Usenet was being used for electronic discussions on a wide variety of topics and soon became a tool for communication. Today, Usenet groups are analogous to a cafe where people from everywhere in the world gather to discuss and share ideas on topics of common interest.

viewer: Programs needed to display graphics, sound, and video. For example, pictures stored as a GIF image have the file name extension ".gif" and need a gif helper application to display the image. Netscape has the required viewers (external helper applications) built into the software. A list of programs required to view files can be found in the Helper Application menu of Netscape. Open the **Options** pull-down menu, select **Preferences**, then **Helper Applications**.

VRML (Virtual Reality Modeling Language): a programming language that makes 3-dimensional virtual reality experiences possible on Web pages.

REFERENCES

Angell, D. (1996, March). The ins and outs of ISDN. *Internet World*, 78-82.

Bennahum, D. S. (1995, May). Domain street, U.S.A. *NetGuide*, 51-56.

Butler, M. (1994). *How to use the Internet*. Emeryville, CA: Ziff-Davis Press.

Career Center (1996). [Online]. Available: http://www.monster.com/home.html
or http://199.94.216.77:80/jobseek/center/cclinks.htm

CareerMosaic Career Resource Center (1996). [Online]. Available:
http://www.careermosaic.com/cm/crc/

Conte, R. (1996, May). Guiding lights. *Internet World*, 41-44.

Dixon, P. (1995, May). Jobs on the web. *SKY*, 130-138.

Ellsworth, J. H., & Ellsworth, M.V. (1994). *The Internet business book*. New York:
John Wiley & Sons, Inc.

Grusky, S. (1996, February). Winning résumés. *Internet World*, 58-68.

Leibs, S. (1995, June). Doing business on the net. *NetGuide*, 48-53.

Leshin, C. (1996). *Internet adventures: Step-by-step guide to finding and using
educational resources*. Boston: Allyn and Bacon.

Leshin, C. (1997). *Netscape adventures: Step-by-step guide to Netscape Navigator
and the World Wide Web*. New Jersey: Prentice Hall.

Miller, D. (1994, October). The many faces of the Internet. *Internet World*, 34-38.

Netscape Communication Corporation. (1996, January/February). *Netscape
Handbook*. [Online]. Currently available by calling 1-415-528-2555 or
online by selecting the Handbook button from within Netscape.

O'Connell, G. M. (1995, May). A new pitch: Advertising on the World Wide Web
is a whole new ball game. *Internet World*, 54-56.

Reichard, K., & King, N. (1996, June). The Internet phone craze. NetGuide, 52-58.

Resnick, R., & Taylor, D. (1994). *The Internet business*. Indianapolis, IN: Sams Publishing.

Richard, E. (1995, April). Anatomy of the World Wide Web. *Internet World*, 28-30.

Riley, Margaret F. (1996). Employement Opportunities and Job Resources on the Internet [Online]. Available: http://www.jobtrak.com./jobguide/

Sachs, D., & Stair, H. (1996). *Hands-on Netscape, a tutorial for Windows users.* New Jersey: Prentice Hall.

Sanchez, R. (1994, November/December). Usenet culture. *Internet World*, 38-41.

Schwartz, E. I. (1996, February). Advertising webonomics 101. *Wired*, 74-82.

Signell, K. (1995, March). Upping the ante: The ins and outs of slip/ppp. *Internet World*, 58-60.

Strangelove, M. (1995, May). The walls come down. *Internet World*, 40-44.

Taylor, D. (1994, November/December). Usenet: Past, present, future. *Internet World*, 27-30.

Timm, P. R. & Stead, J. A. (1996). *Communication skills for business professions.* New Jersey: Prentice Hall.

Vendito, G. (1996, March). Online services—how does their net access stack-up? *Internet World*, 55-65

Venditto, G. (1996, May). Search engine showdown. *Internet World*, 79-86.

Vendito, G. (1996, June). Internet phones—the future is calling. *Internet World*, 40-52.

Weiss, A. (1994, December). Gabfest—Internet relay chat. *Internet World*, 58-62.

Welz, G. (1995, May). A tour of ads online. *Internet World,* 48-50.

Wiggins, R. W. (1994, March). Files come in flavors. *Internet World,* 52-56.

Wiggins, R. W. (1994, April). Webolution: The evolution of the revolutionary World Wide Web. *Internet World*, 33-38.

Wilson, S. (1995). *World Wide Web design guide.* Indiana: Hayden Books.

APPENDIX I
Connecting to the Internet

. . . .

Connecting to the Internet

There are three ways to connect to the Internet:

- a network
- an online service
- a SLIP/PPP connection

Network Connection

Network connections are most often found in colleges, schools, businesses, or government agencies and use dedicated lines to provide fast access to all Internet resources. Special hardware such as routers may be required at the local site. Prices depend on bandwidth and the speed of the connection.

Online Services

Examples of online services include America Online, CompuServe, Prodigy, Delphi, and Microsoft Network. Online services are virtual communities that provide services to their subscribers including electronic mail, discussion forums on topics of interest, real time chats, business and advertising opportunities, software libraries, stock quotes, online newspapers, and Internet resources (Gopher, FTP, newsgroups). There are advantages and disadvantages to these online services.

Advantages

The advantages to online services include:

- easy to install and use,
- content offered by provider,
- easy to find and download software,
- easy-to-use e-mail, and
- virtual community of resources and people.

Commercial online services are excellent places to begin exploring and learning about the use of e-mail and accessing network information and resources.

Disadvantages
The disadvantages to online services include:

- expensive to use,
- do not always access all Internet resources such as Gopher, FTP, and Telnet, and
- must use the online service's e-mail program and Internet browser.

Online services charge an average of $9.95 per month for 5 hours of online time. Additional online time is billed at rates of $2.95 to $5.95 per hour. Some services charge more for being online at peak hours such as during the day.

In comparison, an Internet access provider may charge $15-$30 per month for 100-to-unlimited hours of online time. Prices vary depending on your locality and the Internet access provider.

SLIP/PPP Connection
Internet access providers offer SLIP (Serial Line Interface Protocol) or PPP (Point-to-Point Protocol) connections (SLIP/PPP). This service is referred to as *Dial-Up-Networking* and makes it possible for your PC to dial into their server and communicate with other computers on the Internet. Once you have established a PPP, SLIP, or direct Internet connection, you can use any software that speaks the Internet language called TCP/IP. There are several TCP/IP software applications including Eudora, Netscape Navigator, and Explorer.

Internet service providers should give you the required TCP/IP software to get you connected to the Internet. Additionally, many will provide Internet applications such as Eudora, Netscape Navigator, and Explorer. Prices are usually based on hours of usage, bandwidth, and locality.

TCP/IP and SLIP/PPP Software
Macintosh Software

TCP/IP software for the Macintosh is called MacTCP and is supplied by Apple. Two popular software choices necessary to implement either SLIP or PPP are MacPPP or MacSLIP. Using one of these programs with MacTCP creates a direct Internet connection.

Your Internet access provider should give you software that has already been configured for connecting your Mac to the Internet.

Commercial Online Services
America Online
http://www.aol.com
(800) 827-6347
e-mail: postmaster@aol.com

AT&T WorldNet Services
http://www.att.com
(800) 831-5269
e-mail: webmaster@att.com

CompuServe
(800) 848-8990
e-mail: 70006,101@compuserve.com

Microsoft Network
http://www.msn.com
(800) 426-9400

Prodigy
(800) 776-3449

The WELL
http://www.well.com
(415) 332-4335
e-mail: web-info@well.com

APPENDIX II
Finding an Internet Provider

• •

There are several Web sites to help you find an Internet access provider.

http://thelist.com
http://www.clari.net/iap/iapcode.htm
http://www.primus.com/providers

To find the names of providers in your area, click on the link to your area code. You will find descriptive information of providers in your area code and a description of their services.

NOTE

All providers that service your area will be found by the area code listing.

Tips for Finding a Provider

If your area code is not listed
There are providers who have nationwide access. Some of the Web sites have information on these service providers.

If there is no local dial-in number
Look for service providers that are the closest to you or who have an 800-number dial-in access. Many providers are also listed on these Web sites.

Choosing a provider
Contact providers by phone, fax, or electronic mail. If you want to use Netscape or Explorer you will need to get a SLIP or a PPP account.

Ask about the following:

- Type of Internet accounts available.

- Price and hours of access. How much will it cost per month for a SLIP or PPP account? How many hours of Internet access are included? An average price is $20 per month for 150 hours of graphical access.

- Technical support. Does the provider offer technical support? What are the hours (days, nights, weekends, holidays)? Is support free?

- Software. Do they provide the TCP/IP software? Is the software custom configured? Do they provide free copies of an e-mail program such as Eudora or a Web browser such as Netscape Navigator or Explorer? Good Internet providers will provide custom configured TCP/IP software and the essential Internet navigation and communication software.

NOTE
If you are using Windows 95 you will need to get information for configuring your Windows 95 TCP/IP software. At the time of this printing you cannot get TCP/IP software custom configured for Windows 95.

APPENDIX III
Using an Internet Navigational Suite

• •

Internet front-end navigational suites are complete packages of tools that make it easier for you to connect to the Internet. In the past these suites provided separate software applications packaged together. The newer versions offer integrated software programs that are simple and save time. Every aspect of the Internet is easier, including your initial Internet set-up, Internet navigation, and downloading files using the File Transfer Protocol (FTP).

All of the front-end packages include the following:

• a configuration utility for establishing your Internet service
• e-mail software
• a graphical Web browser
• a newsgroup reader
• an FTP utility

The configuration utility assists you with dialing up a service provider and opening an account. The service providers listed in the software are usually limited to several large companies.

> ## NOTE
> • The cost for an Internet connection provided by the companies listed in front-end suites may be more expensive than the cost of using a local Internet provider.
>
> • Integrated software packages may not allow you to use other e-mail programs or Web browsers.

Suggested Internet Navigational Suites

- EXPLORE Internet: (800) 863-4548
- IBM Internet Connection For Windows: (800) 354-3222
- Internet Anywhere: (519) 888-9910
- Internet Chameleon: (408) 973-7171
- Internet In A Box: (800) 557-9614 or (800) 777-9638
- Netscape Navigator Personal Edition: (415) 528-2555
- SuperHighway Access: (800) 929-3054

APPENDIX IV
How to Reference Electronic Media

At the time of this writing a standard had not yet emerged for referencing online information. The goal of an electronic reference is to credit the author and to enable the reader to find the material. The International Standards Organization (ISO) continues to modify a uniform system of citing electrnic documents. The following guidelines and examples have been compiled from *The American Psychological Association (APA) Publication Manual* and *The Chicago Manual of Style*.

- Be consistent in your references to online documentation or information.
- Capitalization follows the "accepted practice for the language or script in which the information is given."
- Use your discretion for the choice of punctuation used to separate elements and in the use of variations in typeface or underscoring to distinguish or highlight elements.
- If a print form is available and is the same as the electronic form, referencing the print form is preferred.

Include the followingin your reference:

- The author's name if it is available or important for identification.
- The most recent date, if document undergoes revision.
- Title of the document, file, or World Wide Web site.
- Specify the protocol: Telnet, Gopher, FTP, or World Wide Web.
- Provide the Internet address or retrieval path for accessing the information, including the file name, directory, and pathway.
- Do not end a path statement with a period, because it is not part of the Internet address and may hinder retrieval if used.
- If the information is available via a listserv mailing list, provide subscription information.

Format For Referencing Online Information

Author, I. (date). <u>Title of full work</u> [online]. Available: Specify protocol and path.

Author, I., & Author, I. (date). <u>Title of full work</u> [online]. Specify protocol and path.

Examples

World Wide Web

Riley, Margaret F. (1996). Employment Opportunities and Job Resources on the Internet [Online]. Available: http://www.jobtrak.com./jobguide

Gopher

Part I - M.U.S.E. Report (1993, December). [Online]. Available Gopher: gopher://naic.nasa.gov/Pathway: /Guide to NASA Online Resources/ NASA Scientific, Educational, and Governmental Resources/ Government Resources/Americans Communicating Electronically/ Electronic Mail Issues for the FederalGovernment/ Unified Federal Government Electronic Mail Users Support Environment Report

File Transfer Protocol

"History and Philosophy of Project Gutenberg" (1992, August). In Gutenberg Archives [Online].Available FTP: ftp://uiarchive.cso.uiuc.edu Directory: /pub/etext/gutenberg/history.gut

Listserv Mailing List

Smith, J., & Howell, A. (1995, December). "Effective Business Communication." In BUSCOM listserv archives [Online]. Subscribe: Available Listserv archive:

NOTE

A Web site with information on the MLA style for documenting online resources is:
http://www.cas.usf.edu/english/walker/mla.html

INDEX

A

About the Internet option
  Netscape, Directory menu, 22
Add Bookmark option
  Netscape, Bookmarks menu, 19
Address Book option
  Netscape, Window menu, 23
Addresses
 administrative, 90–91
 on Netscape, 11
 server, and URLs, 6
 submission, 90–91
AFRO-American Newspapers, 146
Alta Vista, 65–67, 138
American Carriers Telecommunication
Association (ACTA), 53
America's Job Bank, 112, 126–30
Andreessen, Marc, 9
Applets, 161
ASCII (text) files, 161
Association for Business Communication
 Consultants, 76
AT&T, 78, 144
Auto Load Images option, 21

B

Back option
  Netscape, Go menu, 18
Bank of America, 81
Binary file, 161
Binhex, 161
Bit, 161
Bookmark Items option
  Netscape, Bookmarks menu, 19
Bookmark window, 33
Bookmarks, 161
 adding to a folder, 35–36
 copying, 37
 deleting, 37
 exporting and saving, 37–38

function, 19
importing, 38–39
modifying names of, 36–37
moving, 37
organizing, 33–35
Bookmarks menu. *See* Pull-down menus
Bookmarks option
  Netscape, Window menu, 23
Boolean operators, 58, 161
Browsers, 9–30, 161
Bulletin board system (BBS), 46, 99
Business communication. *See also*
 Internet, Learning activities, and
 World Wide Web
 career planning, 95–104
 finding a job in, 105–134
 learning activities in, 143–59
 Web sites, 73[n]94, 139
Business directories, 134

C

Career planning
 career exploration, 97
 information resources, 98–101,
  103–104
 self-awareness journey, 95–97
Career Web, 112, 132
Chat rooms, 52
Chats
 connecting to, 51–52
 conversations in, 52
 defined, 51
 Web sites of, 52
Chatting, 41
Cities, 130
City Net, 130–31
Clear option
  Netscape, Edit menu, 16
Client, 162
Close option
  Netscape, File menu, 15
CNN, 79, 85
Coles-Dunford-Kimbell, 83
Companies, 119–20, 124–25

Y